CASTLEKNOCK

MEMORIES OF A NEIGHBOURHOOD

SHARING PHOTOGRAPHS:
A hard copy folder of group photos and photos of local landmarks will be made available in due course to the Local History Section of Blanchardstown Library.
These photos will also be available via blogposts on the Wordpress site below where you can log on as a follower if you wish.

reynoldshistorycastleknockblog.wordpress.com

BUYING A COPY OF THIS BOOK:
This book is for sale at the following outlets:-

*Spar, Carpenterstown, Castleknock
*Newsagents, Roselawn S.C., Castleknock
*Centra, Laurel Lodge S.C., Castleknock
*Careys Newsagents, Main St, Lucan
It can also be purchased on-line @ Amazon.com

CASTLEKNOCK

MEMORIES OF A NEIGHBOURHOOD

TONY REYNOLDS

www.carrowmore.ie

First published in Ireland in 2017 by Carrowmore

First edition

Copyright @ Anthony Reynolds, 2017

The right of Tony Reynolds to be identified as the author of this work has been asserted under the Copyright and Related Rights Act, 2000.

All rights reserved. No part of this publication may be reproduced, stored in a retrieval system, or transmitted, in any form or by any means without the prior written permission of the author, nor be otherwise circulated in any from of binding or cover other than that in which it is published and without a similar condition being imposed on the subsequent publisher.

The author acknowledges that there may be errors in this publication. Every effort has been made to verify the contents within the book and the author accepts no responsibility for any inaccuracies.

The author has made all reasonable efforts to identify and contact the original owners of documents and photographs reproduced in this book and acknowledge all copyright holders. In the event of any inadvertent omission, the author will be happy to update future editions of the work in this regard.

The covers of this book feature watercolour paintings by my daughter, Mary. The front cover painting is of our former home on the Carpenterstown Road, at the top of the Sandpits Hill. The shop and the hut had been knocked down at the time of painting, the 'back place,' as we called it, was still there - it is now gone. The back cover shows the Sandpits cottages, which have been very much painted and photographed over the years.

Print edition ISBN: 978-0-9956108-3-5

Carrowmore Publishing
50 City Quay
Dublin 2
www.carrowmore.ie
info@carrowmore.ie

CONTENTS

Prologue		8
Introduction		13
Chapter 1	Reynolds roots in Castleknock	16
Chapter 2	From Castleknock village to Blanchardstown	23
Chapter 3	Our shop - Glen Stores	46
Chapter 4	Castleknock village to our shop	57
Chapter 5	Domestic life	75
Chapter 6	Castleknock National School	81
Chapter 7	Our pets	88
Chapter 8	Along the road to Luttrellstown and the No. 80 bus	93
Chapter 9	Extra-curricular activities	119
Chapter 10	The Coolmine-Clonsilla newspaper run	129
Chapter 11	Outings	153
Chapter 12	The Farmleigh newspaper run	161
Chapter 13	Hallow 'Een and Christmas	174
Chapter 14	The Race-course newspaper run	179
Chapter 15	The War Years	192
Chapter 16	Hunting and grown-up pursuits	201
Chapter 17	Religion	206
Chapter 18	Life after National School	214
Chapter 19	Politics	219
Chapter 20	Night life	221
Chapter 21	Ghostly tales	226
Epilogue		229
Other Reading		231
Acknowledgements		241
About the Author		243

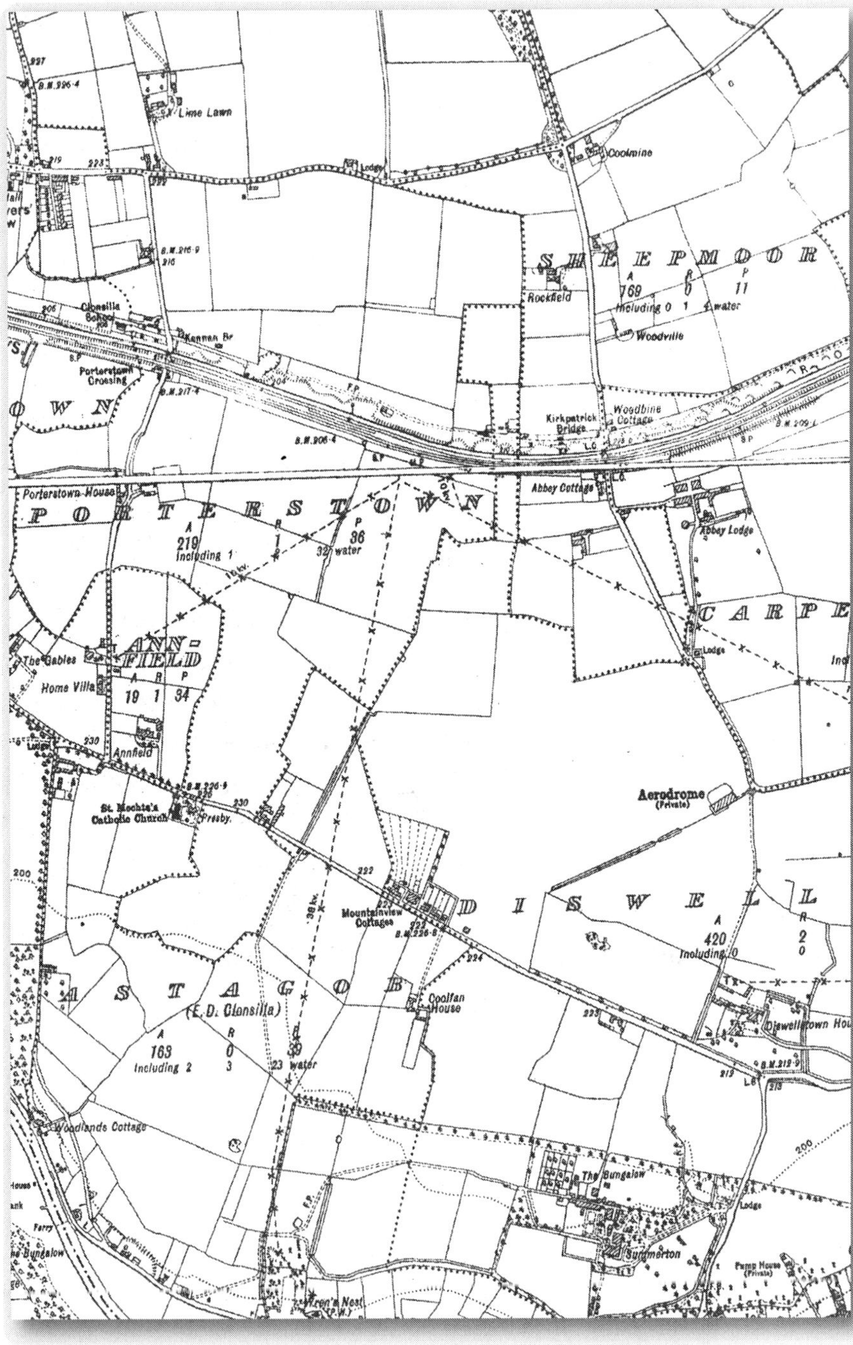

Lime Lawn
Lodge
Coolmine
SHEEPMOOR
Rockfield
Woodville
Clonsilla School
Kennan Br
Porterstown Crossing
Kirkpatrick Bridge
Woodbine Cottage
Porterstown House
PORTERSTOWN
Abbey Cottage
Abbey Lodge
CARPE
Lodge
ANN-FIELD
The Gables
Home Villa
Annfield
St. Mochta's Catholic Church
Presby.
Aerodrome (Private)
Mountainview Cottages
DISWELL
ASTAGOB
(E.D. Clonsilla)
Coolfan House
Diswellstown Hou
Woodlands Cottage
The Bungalow
Lodge
Summerton
Pump House (Private)
Ferry
Wren's Nest

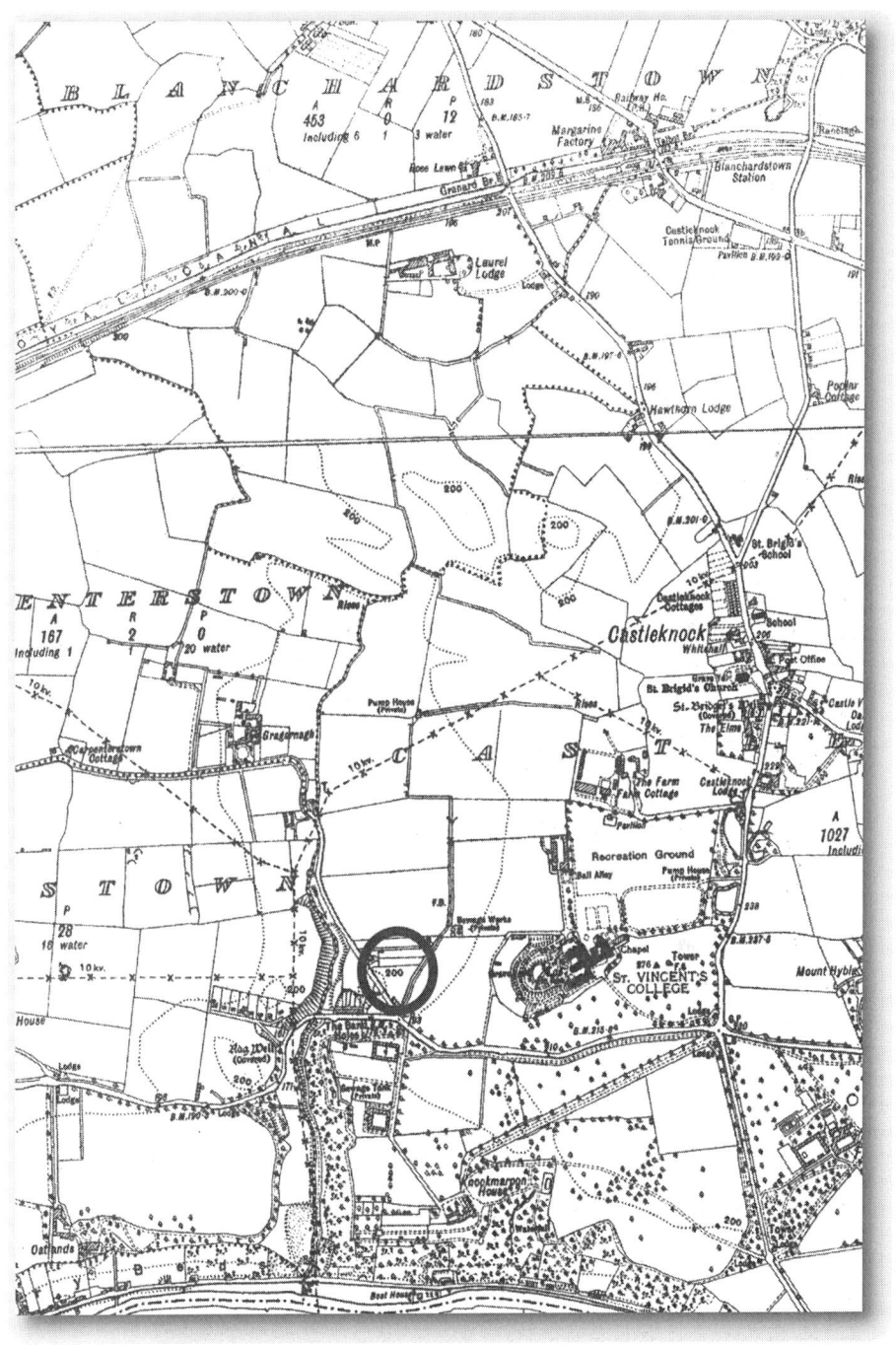

A 1930s view of the neighbourhood of Castleknock. The triangular area highlighted is the former Reynolds family home.

PROLOGUE

The history of Castleknock, Blanchardstown, Strawberry Beds and surrounding areas has been well-documented but in this book my aim is to give a flavour of what it was like growing up in the Castleknock area from the 1930s to the 1970s. I hope to give an insight into peoples' lives, the conditions in which they lived and to reflect on how things meshed together for good and for ill. My family lived at the beating heart of Castleknock, at a point about half way between the village and the Strawberry Beds, in the townland known as Carpenterstown. Our shop, 'Glen Stores,' stood beside our home on over an acre of ground, kept as a market garden. We had relatives in the Sandpits, the Strawberry Beds, Porterstown, Clonsilla, Peck's Lane and Ashtown, and many of our descendants still live in the locality. The Parish Register in Blanchardstown has a record of the Reynolds family extending back to 1758. Given my roots, the shop, and my involvement in local pursuits, I know the social and geographical map more intimately than most people. As I am now in my ninetieth year, I claim a certain authority to write about the locality.

Using the site of our shop as a nucleus, I propose to meander around different roads and outline the social map of the locality, who lived where, who was related to who, and how the community intermingled, a sort of blurring of lines between memoir and social history. I plan to relate my experiences as learned or gleaned. I want to emphasise that these are my personal memories which might differ from those of other family members and neighbours. As in every community, houses and places harbour secrets beneath the placid surface. I have no wish to cause offence in recording events on paper, nor do I wish to offend either by inclusion or omission of people or events. Like everybody else, my memory rests with certain people and events often involving people of my own age - people that others might not consider memorable at all. Before embarking on the journey, I want to highlight some important features that underpinned most communities, as Ireland was a very different place up to the 1970s and the book has to be read in context with the times.

The Irish Constitution of 1937 envisaged the 'family' as one based on marriage alone. Until 1973, women were forced to resign their job on marriage based on the 'marriage bar,' which existed in banks and the Public Service. The idea of equal pay and equal opportunity was only getting an airing in the early 1970s with the Commission on the Status of Women in 1972 setting off campaigns for womens' rights. Legislation on equal pay was introduced in 1974 and employment equality legislation followed in 1977, both as a result of European directives. Contraception for all had not been legalised and until 1987 children born out of wedlock had an 'illegitimate' status. Divorce was rejected by a substantial margin of voters in the first divorce referendum in 1986 - it took ten more years before divorce was signed into law. The power of the clergy was largely unchallenged; people bowed to them as they did with other pillars of the community.

Religion permeated most aspects of life in Ireland and there were essentially two religions, Catholic and Protestant. Not alone did your persuasion tie you together by invisible threads, it also governed your church attendances and spilled over into education and social life. This caused a natural divide in the community, which was innately recognised by all, a case of 'us' and 'them.' One might presume that this worked in reverse too, especially where religious groups were outnumbered. One must also take into consideration that many Catholics referred to certain families as 'Protestant' despite the fact that some were Presbyterian, Methodist, Anglican or of other persuasions.

Another feature was the influence of the local grandee families who provided employment and in many cases, housing. Practically every household in the area had family members that worked at grand houses, on the farm, or engaged as servants, or at establishments such as Castleknock College. The 1911 census shows occupations such as steward, housekeeper, cook, dairyman, herdsman, butler, footman, underservant, valet, maid, coachman, chauffeur, stable hand, gardener or labourer – while most were literate, some were illiterate. As dwelling places often came with a livelihood, many roles were passed down through generations. Others made a living indirectly from these establishments, providing local produce, provisions and services such as horse and cart hire, taxi hire, farm machinery repairs, farrier and veterinary services. Some might say that with this measure of dependency, a certain deference was expected.

As people generally had larger families, they were poorer, often living hand-to-mouth, in tied cottages, or tenanted accommodation. Mortgages or loans were not a feature in the lives of ordinary folk who were paid low wages in cash and who invariably had no bank account and no prospect of ever having one, much less owning their own home. Despite being engaged in low-skilled jobs and the fact that most children only attended school until the age of fourteen, it would be foolish, however, to underestimate their untapped abilities.

On a more local front, certain factors endowed Castleknock with a healthy rate of employment. A preponderance of horses needed to be cared for, given their use on farms as well as in sport - for polo, horse-racing and hunting. Castleknock is proximate to places of employment such as the Phoenix Park, the Ordnance Survey, the railway and to the centre of Dublin, all within cycling distance. The surrounding waterways - the Royal Canal, the Liffey and Tolka rivers – lent themselves to the establishment of factories which gave employment.

The extended Guinness family owned numerous properties in Castleknock ranging from landed gentry estates to tenanted cottages, including Knockmaroon, Glenmaroon, Farmleigh, Luttrellstown Castle Demesne, Castlemount and Oatlands. Members of the extended Laidlaw family lived at Somerton, Diswellstown and Abbey Lodge and the Shackletons had property at Beech Park and Anna Liffey Mill, along the Lower Road. The views from some of these homes extended across the Liffey Valley and the rural landscape beyond, as far as the Wicklow mountains. Back then, Palmerstown and Ballyfermot were all fields, with the exception of a handful of houses and Stewart's Hospital, a multi-storey institution. However, the aftermath of World War II and industrial developments heralded changes to a familiar social landscape. The fall-off in numbers returning to work the land and serve the big house had many repercussions.

In the 1950s, the first housing development was built at Beechpark Avenue and as farms were sold on, estates went up at Woodpark, Roselawn, Hawthorn Lawn, Laurel Lodge and the Georgian village and further out, at Hartstown, Lohunda and Mulhuddart. Castleknock changed almost beyond recognition. The fields where I once hunted are now built upon. The present day primary school and Catholic church are on land adjacent to what was once my grandfather's market garden and the rumble from the M50 motorway can be heard from our old home. I know of a couple living in the area all their lives who got lost in Clonsilla and found their way home by following a number 39 bus.

It is part of life that people break away and although they might end up living not too far away, you may not see them for years. When you bump into them, you can easily re-connect, despite how far you have travelled, because of mutual understanding and that same upbringing in the very marrow of your bones. I felt the need to reach into the past, put pen to paper and record for posterity a way of life around Castleknock that is gone forever.

Castleknock's newer inhabitants cannot be expected to know the one-time importance of landmarks such as 'The Ragwell,' a vital water source, or 'The Glen,' a valuable right of way, 'Clarke's Hill' and 'Daisy Hill,' favourite playing fields, or indeed, 'The Fourteen Trees,' a place that inspired fear, due to its ghostly connections. They are probably not aware either that there was a local vernacular, which manifested itself in people referring to some spinster sisters, for example, as the Miss Breens or the Miss Newenhams, rather than the Misses Breen or Misses Newenham. Also, nicknames abounded to such a degree that people were often known only by nickname and you might never learn their real name at all. A few come to mind: *'Hair Oil'* Nolan, *'Psyche'* Horan, *'Bunsey'* Walker, *'Nukey'* Christian and *'Parky'* Kelly.

INTRODUCTION

A journey from Dublin's O'Connell Bridge down the Quays and along a three mile stretch through the Phoenix Park lands a person in Castleknock. It is a short journey, whether by car, bicycle, or on foot. The bye-law prohibition on commercial traffic through the Phoenix Park was a nuisance in some ways as the bus had to circumvent its outer perimeter, taking a long route by Cabra and along the Navan Road. However, that same bye-law afforded Castleknock a breathing space away from the encroaching metropolis and slowed the urbanisation of the village. Castleknock remained rural, with many making a living from farming or part-time farming, even after the earliest housing estates were built in the 1970s. Until then, it was more or less fields on either side of the road between the Castleknock gate of the Phoenix Park as far as Castleknock village, which comprised a few hundred yards of buildings on either side of the main road.

Castleknock is the anglicised version of Caislean Cnucha, meaning 'Castle on the Hill.' The remains of the Castle still exist on the 'motte' situated in St. Vincent's College grounds but it fell into ruin in the 1700s. Although one belief is that this hill gave its name to Castleknock or Caislean Cnucha as it is known in Irish, there is some evidence that the name is actually derived from a lady called 'Cnucha' who once lived there.

Located eight kilometres west of Dublin, the now suburban village lies in a postal area known as Dublin 15. Our address the world over was: Carpenterstown, Castleknock, Co. Dublin, Ireland. By the 1970s, although Post & Telegraphs (P&T) deliveries had progressed from bicycle to mini-van, the postman had no problem finding the twelve families then living in the townland of Carpenterstown, or the handful of families living in the townland of Diswellstown.

Being rural meant the residents were very much aware of the cycles of nature as well as the agricultural cycle. Not alone was it evident by the activities in the fields but many had family members or neighbours who worked the land. We got around the neighbourhood either walking or cycling. The 'neighbourhood' encompassed distances as far as Dunboyne, Clonsilla, Chapelizod, Inchicore and Clondalkin, the latter two being my workplaces at different times. For trips to town, it was the bike or the bus; very few people had cars. Most engaged Mr. Sheridan's taxi service for special occasions.

The focus in the area was mainly on agriculture with the limestone-rich soil providing excellent cultivation as well as a thriving bloodstock industry. Along the back roads of Castleknock, it was not unusual in the 1970s to see a dairy herd making its way across the public road towards the milking parlour, or to pass steel milk churns left on wooden platforms for collection. In time, the galvanised milk truck ended the need for churns. Until about 1974, cattle auctions were held at Gavin Lowe's market beside Hanlon's Corner. Those riding on the top of a double decker bus could see the menagerie of steel pens inside the mart. The animals either arrived at the city by cattle truck or they were manoeuvred by drovers who kept them overnight in holding fields at Ashtown or penned into yards around Prussia Street. Passersby bore witness to the roars of the animals and bales of hay stacked up as feed. After auction, drovers brought the cattle into small slaughterhouses close to the mart or guided them straight down the North Circular Road and onto the ferry to England. Up until the 1970s, sheep and cattle grazed on a working farm at the junction of Old Cabra Road and New Cabra Road, where housing developments and commercial premises now exist. Until recent times, the Smithfield horse fair - despite being surrounded by apartment blocks - was still held on the first Sunday of every month.

The 1911 census shows that many families in our area took in lodgers, even those who had insufficient accommodation for themselves. Large families and overcrowding were commonplace, especially among Catholics for whom contraception was against the teaching of the church, the Humanae Vitae having decreed in 1968 that artificial contraception in all forms was immoral. Vigorous campaigns resulted in limited availability of contraception in 1980. It was finally made available to all in 1985.

The Shannon Scheme was set up in 1927 and following the erection of electricity poles all over the country, electrification arrived in 1939. After that, there was no more feeling around for a candle or messing with oil and paraffin lamps while trying to find your way in the dark. Out went the 'wireless' too and when gadgets arrived in degrees – electric kettle, cooker, fridge, toaster – you'd wonder how you'd managed before. When mains water arrived in the late 1950s, it changed our lives. With the advent of electricity, telephone, and motor-propelled vehicles, Castleknock acquired a measure of public street lighting, a single telephone coinbox, and a bus stop, all of which are fixtures to this day, except for the telephone kiosk, which is now gone but not forgotten. Many queuing outside in the rain cursed when they spotted the user pushing more coins into the slot to extend the telephone conversation.

Castleknock always had a strong association with horses. The Phoenix Park Racecourse held race meetings regularly and many racehorse trainers were based in Castleknock – Grasswick's stables were beside the Phoenix Park gate and Jim Bolger's stables were beside the Coolmine railway gate. In the early hours, we could hear the skittish trot of racehorses making their way to the gallops in the Phoenix Park. The gallops was a long ploughed strip on 'The Fifteen Acres,' an open area where the Pope's Cross now stands. There were riding schools at Blackhorse Avenue, Deerpark, and at the bottom of the laneway beyond O'Hely's cottage. It was a common sight to see a line of youngsters in hard hats mounted on ponies, following a riding instructor along the road and into the Phoenix Park. Some of the larger houses had a stable and kept a horse or two for private us - for hacking or polo or hunting. The hunt often met in the car park of Myo's Pub.

Castleknock remained a pastoral area until builders bought up farmland for development. Bit by bit, the builders inched their way towards Castleknock until it was finally subsumed into the suburban fabric of Dublin, to the detriment of the character and integrity of the village.

I.
CASTLEKNOCK ROOTS

First off, I'll tell you a bit about myself and how the Reynolds family fit into the scheme of things. My paternal grandparents were Peter Reynolds and Bridget Lovely. Peter Reynolds was a market gardener who lived along what was then known as 'The Side Road' but is long since known as Beechpark Avenue. Bridget Lovely came from the Strawberry Beds. When I was a child, my father climbed up into a ruin between The Glen and the Strawberry Hall and told me that was where his mother had lived. My grandparents had seventeen children, many of whom died in infancy. My father, Patrick Reynolds, known as 'Paddy,' came sixth in the family. The baptismal and burial records are held in Blanchardstown; early entries are in Latin.

The Reynolds family homestead once stood on the site of the present-day Castleknock National School. Their greenhouses were on land behind the house and they owned more land near to Peck's Lane. The house was single-storey, in Tudor style. I was nearly finished national school across the road from this house when I found out my grandparents had lived there at one time. During my school days, the Anderson family lived there – Jimmy Anderson and his brother and sisters were in school with me. I later learned that in 1910, a powerful windstorm swept across Ireland causing severe damage to property and it blew off many a roof. My grandfather's greenhouses were destroyed and his business was ruined. He could not afford to rebuild the greenhouses. Peter died prematurely four years later. His widow, Bridget Reynolds, sold the land piecemeal and moved with her children to rented accommodation in Queen Street. The Registry of Deeds records the sale of land to a local farmer for £265. The reasons why Bridget sold up, went to live in town, and ran out of money are not known.

Tony Reynolds

At the junction of the College Road and Carpenterstown Road, James Reynolds, an ancestor of mine, lived in a thatched cottage on over an acre of ground and paid the rates. A Tudor-style house with Georgian windows eventually replaced the cottage and it still stands there today (see book cover). The red roof tiles have an ornate scalloped capping. The narrow paned windows together with the tall trees opposite make the interior quite dark.

Later on, some unmarried siblings of my grandfather, Peter Reynolds, lived in that house – James, Johnny, Pat and Mary Reynolds. They had a pony and trap and did market gardening. When Mary died, Johnny invited his widowed sister-in-law, my grandmother, Bridget Lovely, to come and keep house. Bridget's younger children, and her brother, Kit Lovely, went to live there too. When all the brothers had died, except for Anthony, who became a British soldier, Bridget was unable to pay the rates. My father, Paddy Reynolds, helped his mother to pay the rates from then on, although by that time he was married with a family and living in rented accommodation at Windsor Terrace, in Portobello.

My father also had a brother Anthony, known as Tony. Having joined the British Army in the 1920s, my uncle Tony rose to the position of Major by the end of World War II. His good shooting skills won him many medals and cups - he eventually became a small guns instructor. On visits home, he stayed in digs or at the Wicklow Hotel and spent time with my father. He used to buy new clothes in Ireland, as rationing continued in England for years after the war. He brought back to England commodities that were scarce there, such as butter. One time, Granny said to Tony, *'When I hadn't heard from you, I was thinking of writing to your Commanding Officer.'* After that, he wrote weekly until Granny died. Eventually, Tony married a lady with apple orchards in Devon and on retirement, he ran a secondary school. You will learn later on that my father had been in the I.R.A. It might seem strange for one brother to be in the British Army and another to be a member of the I.R.A., but it was not that unusual in those days.

My maternal grandparents were Philip Reilly and Frances Kavanagh. It is said that my grandfather's family lived at one stage in the yard of a grand house at Dunsink, before moving to a place called 'The Two Yards' near Laurel Lodge. I knew some of the families who lived in the three or four cottages at 'The Two Yards,' including Jimmy ('Duffer') Fleming, a strong fellow, who went to school with me. Mr. Spaine, the shoemaker, had a workshop at the Two Yards; I went to school with his sons, who all had blonde hair. The dwellings in the yard surrounded a grassy square patch on which farm carts were stored, their shafts in the air.

McCarthy's bungalow was later built on that site. My maternal grandparents later moved to a cottage at Ashtown which stood directly across the road from the present entrance of St. Vincent's Centre on the Navan Road. They had eight children that survived infancy. My mother, Helen Reilly, was one of the younger ones. My grandfather worked in the Zoo. My Aunt Jen remained on in that cottage with her husband, Ned, who used to look after cattle held in surrounding fields, in readiness for the mart.

In about 1910, my father, Paddy Reynolds, worked after school hours as a telegraph delivery boy, out of the Castleknock Telephone Exchange. When he left school at the age of fourteen, he started serving his time as a gardener at Robert Emmet's house in Rathfarnham, but he then abandoned gardening. He worked as a waiter in the Wicklow Hotel for fifty years. The hours were long – once every three weeks he had a seven o'clock start and many a time, he didn't finish until eleven o'clock at night. Many late nights he cycled home through the Phoenix Park in all weathers and returned to work the following morning at 7.00 a.m., either by bicycle or bus. The odd time, he missed the last bus and had to get an IOC bus along the Navan Road as far as Peck's Lane and walk home. When I got a car in my twenties, I used to drop him off or collect him, when I could, as he was getting on in years. The retirement age at the time was 70. While there, he made many friends and seemed to be well-liked. A work colleague wrote this poem for a staff bash one Christmas.

We've worked like slaves the whole year round, we've done our best each day.
But now it's party time again and tonight we're all going gay.
Our skipper Jackie Gaffikin will dance and sing and shout.
He got tired of showing people in, so tonight he's showed them out.

Des got tired of serving wines, he thought he'd show some sense.
So he let the girls off tonight and took over the dispense.
Uncle Jer, our favourite baritone will not be out of sorts
For there won't be any bills tonight, so he won't have any shorts.

For Paddy Forde and Willie Browne the night will be a whirl.

They'll enter in the 'Lucky Dip' to see who'll get a girl.
We're sorry Larry couldn't come, he's broken all the rules.
But he had to hurry home tonight to do his weekly pools.

Our two good friends O'Dowd and Doyle will be a happy pair.
And if Jimmy had his budgie here, he wouldn't have a care.
When you sit at home next Sunday, to the radio please tune-in.
To hear appeals from Paddy Reynolds for us to pay our union.

When at last it's time to going home and we've had a happy time.
We'll get a lift in Kirley's car, if it's pushed by Paddy Ryan.
So our thanks to Miss McCrossan and to Miss O'Malley too.
A very Merry Christmas and a Happy New Year too.

My mother, Helen Reilly, was brought up at Ashtown, across from St. Vincent's on the Navan Road. She attended the national school in the Phoenix Park and left at the age of fourteen. Her older sister, Fanny, took her to start service at Millicent House in Co. Kildare, which was then owned by Sir Basil Goulding. She lasted about two weeks, having been turned off by the task of cleaning out chickens. Her next job was in a shoe polish factory at Ashtown where she worked until her marriage. It was said that her mother found it hard to let her daughters go, so my mother married without telling my grandmother, Frances Reilly. I only found this out after my mother died.

After their marriage, my parents rented the downstairs portion of a house at Windsor Terrace, near Harold's Cross Bridge. My mother told me they liked the convenience of Windsor Terrace because she had running water and a gas supply. It was also near to the shops and within walking distance of the Wicklow Hotel.

Our neighbours upstairs were the Camlin family. Mrs Camlin was a widow with five children. Willie was in the RAF and he died in a plane crash over the Irish sea. Freddie was seemingly recovering from tuberculosis and planning to join the Palestinian Police for the climate, when TB took him. The youngest, Fanny, married, but Violet and Gladys never married. This aside about the Camlin family shows how at that time, a family could quickly dissipate because of health troubles, war and for other reasons.

Castleknock – Memories of a Neighbourhood

My first memory is riding a pedal car along the canal path at Portobello. Whenever the pedals stuck, the Camlin boys used to fix it by turning it upside-down and releasing the pedals. Another memory is fishing with my father, using a worm tied by thread onto a piece of stick, and collecting pinkeens in a net.

When my grandmother, Bridget Reynolds, invited my parents to live with her at Carpenterstown, Bridget's daughters, my aunts, Josie Reynolds and Aggie Reynolds, were still living there as well as her brother, Kit Lovely. By the time we moved in with them in 1932, my parents had three children, Maureen, Carmel, and myself. Josie Reynolds and Aggie Reynolds moved into a cottage in Weaver's Row, Clonsilla and lived there until they married.

Reilly sisters, from top left: Genevieve Smith, Helen Reynolds, Mary Reilly, Maggie Reilly. Courtesy Reynolds Family Private Collection.

I remember my grandmother as a nice woman who regularly walked the five

My sister Carmel in my pedal car. Courtesy Reynolds Family Private Collection.

miles into Dublin city centre. She was in her sixties when our family came to live with her in Castleknock and she died in 1933/1934. I have a memory of her hoeing vigorously in the garden, doing it better than me. Even when she acceded to my request to swop hoes, I was surprised that she was still better able to hoe than me. The morning Granny died, Maureen and myself were jumping on the bed when my father came in and shushed us. There was a lot of comings and goings that day and people calling so we knew that something grave had happened.

When we were older, we learned that Granny had been getting out of bed that morning when she had a heart attack, fell back onto the bed and died. She was only sixty-three.

My parents went on to have three more children who survived - Noel, Dolores and Geraldine. An older brother, Charlie, died of diphtheria in infancy. My mother gave birth to all her babies in Holles Street, except the youngest, Geraldine, who was born in the Rotunda Hospital. My father died in 1969 and my mother died in 1979.

Patrick (Paddy) Reynolds & Helen Reynolds with children Charlie and Maureen. Courtesy Reynolds Family Private Collection.

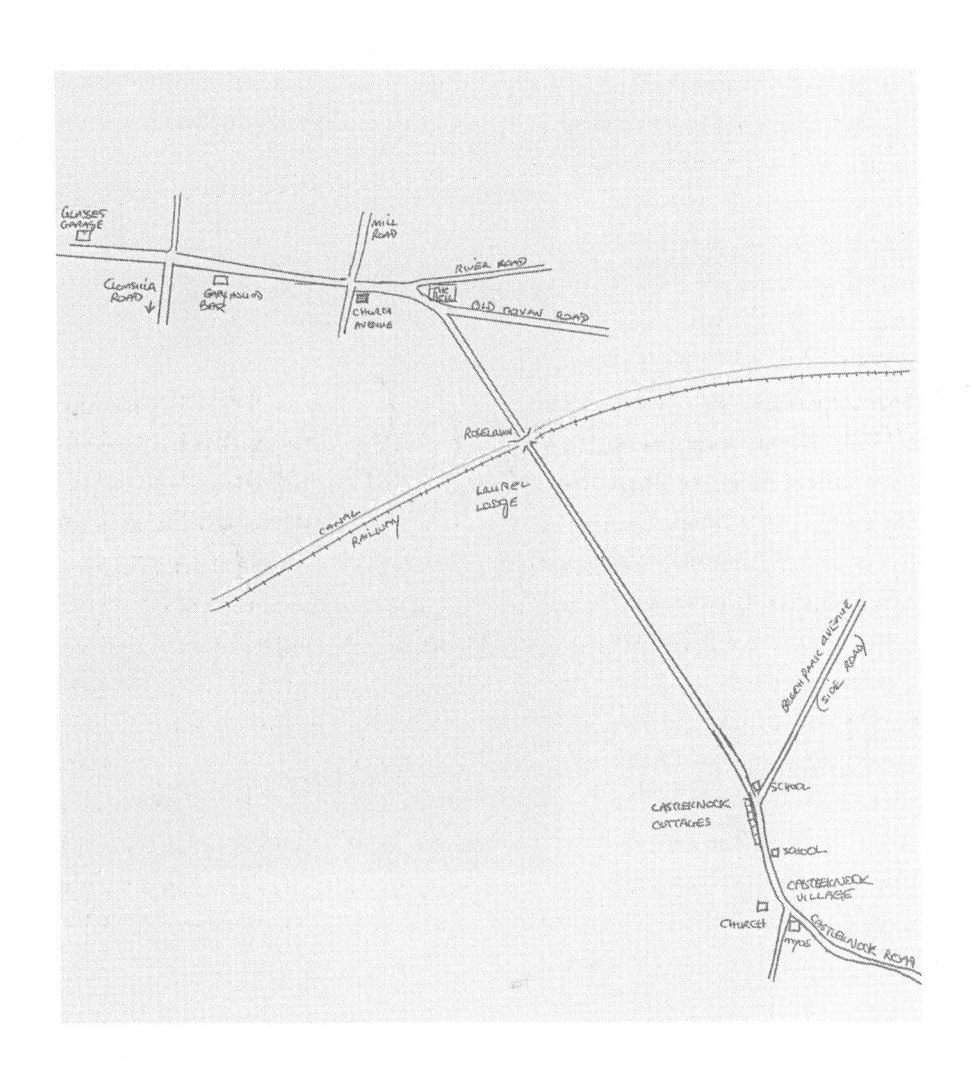

2.
FROM CASTLEKNOCK VILLAGE TO BLANCHARDSTOWN

St Brigid's Church, Castleknock. Courtesy Reynolds Family Private Collection.

The foundation stone of St. Brigids, Church of Ireland, Castleknock, was laid in 1803 on the site of an old Abbey. In May 1177, Henry II and Hugh de Lacy granted 12,001 acres of land in Castleknock to Hugh Tyrell, first Baron of Castleknock. A copy of the charter of the grant in Latin was discovered in 1933 by Eric St. John Brooks in the London Public Records Office. In 1185, Richard Tyrell, son of Hugh Tyrell, gave a grant to the Benedictine monks from the Abbey of Little Malvern in Worcestershire to endow a religious house in Castleknock in honour of St. Brigid. They founded a monastery beside St. Brigid's Well called the Abbey of St. Brigid in Castleknock and it was a dependent priory of Little Malvern. The lands and priory were transferred to the ownership of St. Mary's Abbey in 1486 and on the dissolution of the monasteries after Henry VIII broke with Rome, it became the property of the Luttrell family. The first church was built here in 1609 on the site of the monastery of St. Brigid. In 1803, the foundation stone was laid by Hans Hamilton for the re-building of St. Brigid's, the present day Protestant church in Castleknock. The oldest building in Castleknock, surrounded by high walls and a graveyard, this church is at the heart of the village. Its vibrant Harry Clarke window ('the Brooke window') was commissioned in 1926 by the Brooke family, former residents at Somerton. The church spire was removed in the 1950s following fire damage, having been struck by lightening.

With the exception of the chapel in Castleknock College, there was no Catholic church in the village until one was built off Beechpark Avenue in 1983. Mostly, Catholics attended the 'mother church' in the parish, St. Brigid's Church in Blanchardstown, built in 1837, or St. Mochta's Church in Porterstown, built in 1890 as a 'chapel of ease.' While some Catholics found it more convenient to attended Mass in Castleknock College, there was often a clampdown at the behest of the parish priest in Blanchardstown, who was at the loss of donations. To clarify, there are two churches and three schools in the area, all called St. Brigid's – the Protestant church

Harry Clarke window in St Brigid's Church, Castleknock.

and national school in Castleknock, the Catholic church and national school in Blanchardstown and the school in Castleknock.

At the heart of Castleknock village is Myo's pub, which was previously owned by Ger McKenna. In Ger McKenna's time, it was a spit-and-sawdust pub with a snug, the latter being the only place suitable for a man to bring his wife or ladyfriend for a drink. "*No ladies allowed*," was the usual notice displayed in pubs at that time. While this pub had no specific notice, the rule was more or less observed.

McKenna's Pub, now Myo's, Castleknock village. Photograph accessed in Blanchardstown Library on 26/11/2016. Courtesy of Fingal County Libraries.

Photograph of Castleknock village, c. 1900. Accessed in Blanchardstown Library on 26/11/2016. Courtesy Fingal County Libraries.

Castleknock – Memories of a Neighbourhood

The pub was sold on to Myo O'Donnell, a nephew of Peter Kelly, who owned the Halfway House at Ashtown, where Myo had served his time as a barman. At that stage, the pub was essentially a double fronted house with family quarters upstairs and the licensed premises on the ground floor.

Two whitewashed thatched cottages once stood back from the road in what is now Myo's car park – they were located in the far corner, away from the pub. The Cassidys lived in one of the cottages, 'Rose Cottage.' Pat Cassidy was in school with me; he was a hard-working fellow, who undertook jobs after school. While at national school in the 1930's, Marie Cassidy made a handwritten contribution to the Schools Folklore Collection. Although I remember the buildings between the pub premises and

Public Telephone sign. Courtesy Little Museum of Dublin.

the two cottages that once housed a forge, the forge was not operative in my time. My father remembered the working forge beside the pub, and also, the cottages shown in the photographs that once backed onto the wall of the Protestant Church.

L to R: Former Brownes' home, Penny Bank and Telephone Exchange, Castleknock village. Courtesy Reynolds Family Private Collection.

Directly across the road from Myo's, a pair of semi-detached two-storey buildings, housed a Telephone Exchange and a bank. The Miss Cassidys lived in the house on the right, from where they operated the Telephone Exchange, assisted by their nephew in their later years. As well as the Postal Telegraph Office, it accommodated a Telephone Exchange Call Office, where members of the public could place calls on the telephone provided. 'The Penny Bank' was also founded here by Sir Hugh Mahon who persuaded his Guinness relations to join forces; it became the Guinness & Mahon Bank.

The Browne family and their four sons lived in Ennis House, to the left of the post office and bank buildings. Mrs. Browne's maiden name was Drake. I cannot recall the name of the eldest brother but I knew the younger brothers well – 'Bendy' Browne, Gerald and Kevin. Kevin Browne was in my class at school. He was clever; he taught himself piano and became a superb pianist. He played piano at functions for charity and he was involved in local dramatics. The Brownes belonged to Castleknock Lawn Tennis Club, which was membership by invitation only. Kevin Browne married Josie Kane from Clonsilla, who once partnered me in badminton doubles. They went to live in the second house down on the Rugged Lane. Kevin was a

Molloy's former shop, Castleknock village. The Oratory was to the left and the bookies at the back, in through the gate. Courtesy Reynolds Family Private Collection.

successful salesman with McCairn's Motors; he was instrumental in securing the sale of a new fleet of patrol cars to the police force. 'Bendy' Browne married a sister of Jackie Egan from Peck's Lane who was in school with me.

A single petrol pump and wooden shack once stood on the site of the present day petrol station. Kevin Browne was involved in running the petrol station and 'Bendy' used to serve the petrol. On occasion when you went for a refill, it was shut and you'd have to go elsewhere.

Directly across the road from the Church, which we called 'the Protestant Church,' the Molloy family had a grocery shop with a bookie shop tucked in behind. Mrs. Molloy was formerly a Corcoran and her sister was married to the butcher in Blanchardstown, Patrick O'Reilly. Mr. Molloy was also a bookmaker and used to stand at the racecourse. Much later on, the Walsh family ran the shop. Before the Catholic church was built in Castleknock village, a room adjacent to the shop was used as an oratory where parishioners could call in to say a prayer. A florist now occupies the shop premises.

Alongside Molloy's, a shop and Post Office were housed in red-brick buildings. You took a step back in time when you crossed the granite threshold to the

Former Castleknock Post Office. Courtesy Reynolds Family Private Collection.

ring of a bell and stood on the bare floorboards inside. Stock still, not a sound; you wondered when somebody would come. On the right, a counter stretched the full length of the shop. A sheet of frosted glass divided the Post Office at the front from the shop end. With provisions stacked on open shelves up to the ceiling, a step ladder was often needed to retrieve goods.

The Breens ran the Post Office for years, ably assisted by Miss Jane Meade, who came to work there in 1946. Miss Mary Breen worked in the Post Office until her nineties and on her retirement, Miss Meade took over. After Miss Meade retired, she used to walk her angry-looking dog. The Post Office business was transferred into a shop opposite Myo's pub and eventually, the old red-bricked post office building was sold on for development.

Our usual postman was Billy Bryan, who delivered by bicycle. There was also a full-time postmistress, Sarah Toole, who rode an oversized pushbike. Both of them lived in Castleknock cottages opposite the Protestant school. At Christmas, one or two young school boys on bikes were taken on to help with the extra load and sometimes, Maggie Clarke did deliveries. There was a bit of a hoo-ha one Christmas when some Christmas cards were discovered thrown over a hedge, the result of too many whiskey offerings along the post route, it was said.

L to R: Former homes of Ennis and Sexton/Higgins families. Courtesy Reynolds Family Private Collection.

Castleknock – Memories of a Neighbourhood

L to R: Former homes of Plunkett/Donegan and Maher/Ennis families. Courtesy Reynolds Family Private Collection.

It is hard to believe that up until the 1980s, there was only Molloy's shop and the Post Office-cum-shop in Castleknock. The nearest supermarket was behind the Greyhound Bar in Blanchardstown, until Mogensen's opened in between the Protestant school and Dr. Nelson's house. That premises is now part of the Castleknock Centre.

The Guinness family owned a pair of semi-detached red-brick houses next to the Post Office. The Sextons lived in the house nearest to the Post Office. Mr. Sexton was the sexton in the Protestant church across the road and he dug the graves. Mr. Sexton's daughter married a Mr. Higgins, who later became the sexton. Paddy Ennis lived next door.

The next semi was occupied by the Maher family and later, the Ennis family; the house is now used as a business. In the last house, a Mr. Donegan lived with his wife, whose maiden name was Plunkett. Mrs. Donegan was maternal grandmother to my Reynolds' cousins in Peck's Lane.

An avenue beyond Donegans' leads to a house called 'Glenmalure.' Next is a detached house, 'Sadleir's Field,' a name perhaps associated with the former rector, the Reverend Ralph Sadleir. Alongside this row of houses is St. Brigid's primary

Kilbride House. Courtesy Reynolds Family Private Collection.

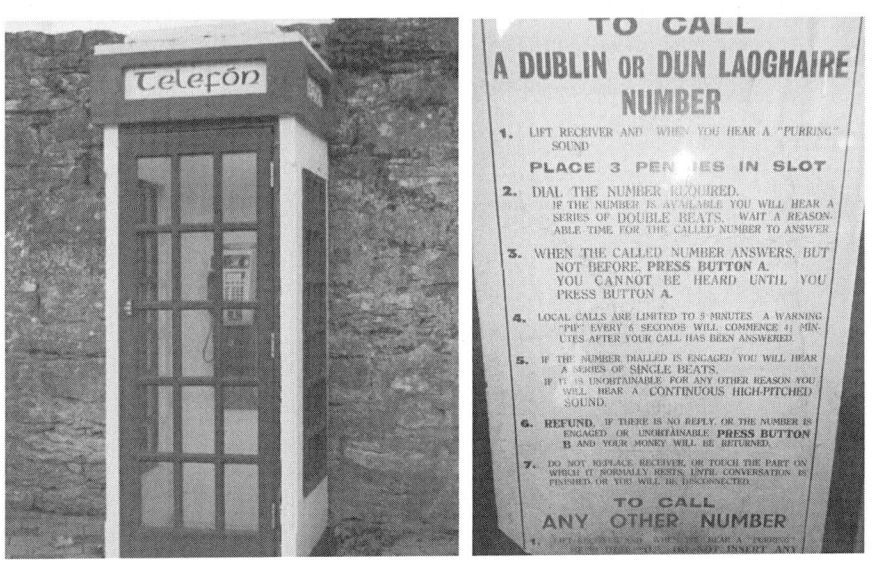

Left: former Post & Telegraphs telephone box, Castleknock village. Right: instructions for using a Public Telephone were affixed inside all telephone boxes. Photos courtesy Reynolds Family Private Collection.

school, which we called 'the Protestant school.' A school was originally opened here in 1720 but the present-day building opened in 1962. Beside the school is the Castleknock Parish Centre and a house, 'Kilbride,' where to my recollection, Archbishop Buchanan lived in retirement.

Back on the church side of the road, the only public telephone kiosk in the village backed onto the church wall. Gaffneys' cottage was right beside the bus stop – it had a pedestrian gate. People used to cycle as far as Castleknock and leave their bikes in behind the hedge at Gaffneys' wall before catching the bus to town. Andy Hill ran a barber-shop in wooden buildings in the yard behind Gaffney's cottage. I used to go to him for a haircut every few weeks but never on a Saturday, because the queue was too long. Many farmers went to Andy for a hot shave with a cut-throat razor on Saturdays; the shave was so close, they wouldn't need to shave for a few days. Some members of the Hill family still run barber businesses in the locality. A housing development, 'The Heathers,' was built on Gaffneys' land. The Guards' barracks, which covered the Blanchardstown and Clonsilla localities as well as Castleknock, was next to Gaffneys.' Eventually the barracks moved in 1935 to Main Street, Blanchardstown, beside the petrol station. Guard Corcoran was our local guard but there was little crime apart from someone being charged for not having a light on their bicycle or a farmer being prosecuted for having ragwort growing in their field. I knew of nobody involved in crime, although I am sure petty thievery and salmon poaching went on, with nobody making a living from either.

The Horgan brothers lived in a pair of red-bricked semi-detached houses alongside the barracks. Dr. Horgan was a doctor of science and one of the few people in the area with a car. For about two years into the war, he continued to run his car on gas, until the Government cut fuel supplies even further. An apartment complex called Donn-Rua now stands on the site of their homes.

Next is a row of cottages, 'Castleknock Cottages.' I shall try and recall the occupants from my early days and hope that memory serves me correctly. The first cottage was occupied by the Scallys; I was in school with Leo Scally who had a younger sister, May. A younger brother whose name I cannot recall, stayed on living there after Leo and May had left. Mrs. Scally did housekeeping for the racehorse trainer, the 'Rasher' Byrne, whose establishment was located around where the Chesterfield housing estate now stands. Una Coyle and her family were in the next cottage; Winnie Coyle was in school with me and made a contribution to the Schools Folklore Collection in the 1930s. Winnie sadly died shortly after leaving school. Next door was Mr. Drake, a brother of Mr. Drake in the Sandpits. Mrs. O'Connor also lived along there with her children, Renee, Benny, and Joseph ('Josie'), the latter who was in my class at school. Mrs. O'Connor worked in the College and the boys used to go up to her there after school to play handball. When Renee O'Connor married, she lived in one of the newer detached houses along College Road. Mrs. Ennis lived in number 6 and Mr. Toole, father of Sarah Toole, who delivered post, lived in number 7. Billy Bryan, the postman, lived in the last house with his wife – they had no children. After our half-hour lunch at school, the master used to detail two of the lads to pick up leftover crusts of bread in the yard with their bare hands and bring them over to the Bryans, as feed for their hens.

Maggie Clarke was an oldish woman who lived in a cottage opposite Castleknock School. A relation of hers who used to visit was a person of interest to us young lads, because he was in the French Foreign Legion. It surprised us that he was allowed to come home on visits because of the Legion's tough reputation and the myth that once you signed up, you could never get out.

A man known as "the Captain" lived in a small cottage with its gable end to the road, directly across the road from our school. Perhaps it was his habit of wearing a peaked captain's hat and his limp that gave him the nickname, but he was not a seafaring man at all.

Castleknock cottages, Castleknock village. Courtesy Reynolds Family Private Collection.

Castleknock – Memories of a Neighbourhood

Castleknock cottages, Castleknock village. C. 1900. Accessed in Blanchardstown Library. Courtesy Fingal County Libraries.

A smart Protestant man, Mr. Smyth, had a farm where Oaklawn and Park Drive are now located. His daughter used to drive a pony and cart with milk churns on the back. She always dressed in trousers and wellington boots and I can see her in my mind's eye now, urging on the pony with a stick. The old national school that my family attended stood on the left hand corner of what we knew as the 'Side Road,' now formally named 'Beechpark Avenue.' An apartment block now stands on this site. Later on, Dr. Nelson came to live in a house called 'Wendover' on the opposite corner of Beechpark Avenue and had his surgery there. 'Wendover' apartment block is there now.

The new national school on the opposite side of the road was built in the vicinity of the market garden once owned by my paternal grandparents. The new Catholic Church was later built beside the school.

Dr. Haldene Nelson's telephone entry. Photograph extract, 1954 Telephone Directory. Directory Courtesy of Little Museum of Dublin.

The Pembertons lived in an imposing bungalow further on towards the Navan Road. I remember them always being smartly dressed. John Pemberton was a class below me in school.

Castleknock Lawn Tennis club, in existence since the 1920s, is at the Navan Road end of Beechpark Avenue. The club was first registered with the Irish Lawn

Castleknock Lawn Tennis Club. Courtesy Reynolds Private Family Collection.

Tennis Club in 1934 with '*Mr. T.J. Browne, Ennis House, Castleknock,*' listed as Honorary Secretary. Opposite the tennis club, Farmhand carried on an agricultural machinery business from 1972 to 2008, when it moved to Damastown.

Nearby is 'The High Bridge,' as we called it, over the Royal Canal at the 12th lock. The Duke of Leinster was a chief backer of the Royal Canal as he wanted the canal to pass near his estate, Carton Demesne, in Maynooth. During the war, the canals were used to transport turf in barges. However, this practice petered out after the war with the development of rail transport. The canal was under the

Barge on Royal Canal. Courtesy Fingal County Council.

Castleknock – Memories of a Neighbourhood

control of CIE from 1944, until it was officially closed to navigation in 1951. A flour mill operated along the canal from the 1800s and used the waterway facility to transport grain. In the early 1900s, this became the British Margarine Factory and although Crest Foods took it over in 1972, we always knew it as 'the margarine factory.' Following a fire around 1984, the premises was sold on and developed into The Mill apartments.

Paddy Donnelly's public house near the High Bridge on the Navan Road was formerly called 'Railway House.' The Blanchardstown Chronicle of 31st of December 1938 records an entry for 'John Donnelly, Proprietor, Railway Hotel,' in the 1930 Post Office Directory. The premises later became The Bridge House and eventually, a bicycle shop, Bridge Cycles, was set up in the premises. The building was demolished to make way for the Talbot Court housing estate. The Donnellys then opened another pub down the road called The Twin Oaks, later re-named.

Let me take you back to the corner of Beechpark Avenue and the Castleknock Road and on towards Blanchardstown. The Finn family owned land from the national school along the stretch of road towards Blanchardstown. Their house,

Donnelly's public house, Navan Road, Blanchardstown, c. 1970s. Photograph accessed in Blanchardstown Library on 26/11/2016. Courtesy Fingal County Libraries.

known locally as 'Finn's yard,' was located at the present day entrance to Hawthorn Lawn. There were always horses and carts in the yard. The original house was replaced by a bungalow which is still there, beside the roundabout that serves Park Drive and Hawthorn Lawn. Kathleen Clarke's mother was formerly a 'Finn' who lived there before she settled in the cottage opposite us in Carpenterstown. The Henry family built a house beside the Finns that now stands next to the motorway. Hawthorn Lawn was developed in the 1970s and was followed by another development called Hawthorn Lodge.

The opposite side of the road to Finn's land was also fields. On the left, beyond where the M50 passover towards Blanchardstown is now, was a place known as 'The Two Yards' where my mother's people, the Reillys, once lived. Mr. Spaine, the cobbler, had his workshop there and a notice outside said, 'Support home industry and send your boots to Spaine.' He lived with his family in Peck's Lane. Past the 'Two Yards,' just before the railway and canal bridge, was a grand house surrounded by fields - Laurel Lodge - belonging to the Brady family. It was known as 'Brady's Farm.' The gate lodge was home to Guard Corcoran. The house was demolished and several housing estates were built on the surrounding farmland: Laurel Lodge, Parklands, Maple, Bramley, Oaktree, Cherry, Sycamore and Laverna estates.

On the opposite side of the road, the Corcoran family farm, Crevlin, colloquially known as "The Bridge," was about 35 acres in size. Thomas Corcoran also owned a public house in Blanchardstown, which later became Davy & Phelan's

The Misses Corcoran, outside their pub and shop, since called Davy & Phelan's, then The Bell. Courtesy Reynolds Family Private Collection.

Castleknock – Memories of a Neighbourhood

Crevlin Farm owned by the Corcoran family, showing Mary McCaughey, who assisted Mrs. Corcoran in raising her family. Courtesy Blanchardstown-Castleknock Historical Society.

and still exists today as "The Bell." Josephine Corcoran married Patrick O'Reilly, who had the butcher shop in Blanchardstown. Up the canal bank to the left, a track led to Sally Gardens, where the Hughes family lived. Some of the Hughes children wrote folklore pieces for The Schools Collection.

Granard Bridge, over the Royal canal and railway, always marked the boundary between Castleknock and Blanchardstown. When new developments at Roselawn, Woodlawn and Brompton were sold by the builder with a Castleknock address, a row about postal deliveries ensued with the Post Office. The row culminated in the old Castleknock boundary being stretched to accommodate the new developments.

The Manleys of Abbey Lodge in Carpenterstown sold up and moved to Roselawn House, which was in the Georgian style, backing onto the canal. Joe Manley was a gentleman jockey and a successful trainer of many winners. The Manley and Brady families were noted for their bloodstock; both families reared war horses for use by the British Army. On towards Blanchardstown and the Bell public house, formerly known as Davy & Phelan's and before that again, Corcoran's pub. The Blanchardstown Chronicle of 31st of December 1938 records an entry for 'Thomas Corcoran, vintner,' in the 1930 Post Office Directory.

The RIC barracks in Blanchardstown was blown up in 1922, before I was born. When I was at national school, the Guards' barracks in Castleknock was the only barracks in the locality. On 27th of September 1935, a new barracks

Brien's Forge, Blanchardstown, c. 1920s. The forge was located on the corner of Main Street and the Clonsilla Road, where a Chinese takeaway now stands. Courtesy Fingal County Libraries

Junction of Castleknock Road at Blanchardstown. (A Guard lived there in the house on the far right, in my time). Photograph accessed in Blanchardstown Library on 26/11/2016. Courtesy of Fingal County Libraries.

opened beside the garage on Main Street, Blanchardstown and the barracks in Castleknock closed. An article in the Blanchardstown Chronicle of 31st of December 1938 mentions that the site for the new station had been bought from Mrs. Carr for £100. The article documents that the Duty Sergeant was then Patrick Kavanagh and other personnel included James Dillon, M. Donovan, Edmond Corbett, James Ledwith and Hugh McDonnell. It would not have been

Castleknock – Memories of a Neighbourhood

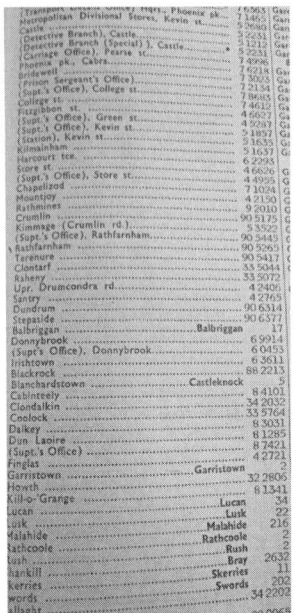

Left: list of barracks telephone numbers showing Blanchardstown as Castleknock 5. Telephone Directory Courtesy of Little Museum of Dublin. Right: the Royal Irish Constabulary (RIC) barracks in Blanchardstown, blown up in 1922. Photograph accessed in Blanchardstown Library on 26/11/2016. Courtesy of Fingal County Libraries.

unusual back then for some of the Guards to live on the premises. That same copy of the Blanchardstown Chronicle also records 1930 Post Office Directory entries: 'William Carr, farmer,' and 'Mrs. W. Carr, sub-postmistress.' In 1990, a new barracks was built at the end of the Clonsilla Road in Blanchardstown. The old barracks on Main Street is now an Adult Education Centre.

O'Reilly's family butcher was built on the site of the old RIC barracks at the entrance to the River Road; the bolts for the steel shutters are still in the window sills. T.P. O'Reilly – an only son with several sisters – started at St. Brigid's National School in Castleknock on the same day as me. When he was about sixteen, T.P.'s father died, which meant T.P. had to take over the business. People remember him bidding for cattle at the mart at that young age. He married Madge, whose father was a cattle dealer. His elder sister, Kitty, married Dr. Cullen's son, also a doctor, but she was widowed young. Another sister older than me, called 'Paddy', was a nurse. Betty married Peter Kelly, the publican of the Half Way House. In the 1930s, Monica O'Reilly wrote a piece about Blanchardstown for The Schools Collection. T.P. eventually relocated the butcher shop near to Godley's drapery shop on Main

T.P. O'Reilly's Victuallers, Blanchardstown, c. 1930's (T.P. O'Reilly as a child). Photograph accessed in Blanchardstown Library on 26/11/2016. Courtesy of Fingal County Libraries.

Street, Blanchardstown, opposite the Greyhound pub. The old butcher premises remains intact and it now houses a florist business and solicitor's practice. T.P. is now sadly gone.

Connolly's Hall, alongside the old butcher shop, was used for community meetings and the children's matinee on Saturday, which I often attended with my sister Maureen or friends. The matinee featured film shows with the likes of *Buster Keaton*, who did comedy with a deadpan expression, or *Tom Mix*, who was the star of many silent Westerns, or cartoons, such as *Tom and Jerry* and *Mickey Mouse*.

Next was the old Post Office, a narrow building with the Post Office section at the back and a shop at the front. The shop was run by Una Caulfield, who also assisted the postmistress. One time, burglars got into the Post Office by drilling a hole through a back wall; cheeky, given its proximity to the Guards' Barracks.

The corner shop owned by M & K Doyle at Church Avenue was in the family for generations. It sold everything from fuel to groceries. Across the road from Doyle's shop was Ryan's garage, which was run by Tim Ryan for years.

In my time, there were two forges in Blanchardstown. The bigger forge, Brien's

Blanchardstown's Old Post Office on Main Street located where the SVP shop is at Deanstown House Centre. Photograph courtesy of Blanchardstown-Castleknock Historical Society and Boards.ie.

stood at the junction of the Main Street and the Clonsilla Road. When the forge was well gone, the site accommodated a galvinised tin shop, run by 'Justin,' a well-known shopkeeper, who later opened a fruit and vegetable shop down the

Blanchardstown Main Street, c. 1900, showing Doyle's corner shop. Photograph accessed in Blanchardstown Library on 26/11/2016. Courtesy of Fingal County Libraries.

road. A Chinese restaurant is now located on the site. The smaller forge was in a row of cottages beyond a wide grass verge opposite the Greyhound pub. The farrier had a moustache and always wore a soft hat. My father knew him as they were both Fianna Fail men. Those cottages have since been replaced by a row of double-fronted bay window bungalows. Another forge in Clonsilla was run by the Hughes family.

The Glass family had a garage a bit beyond the junction of the Clonsilla Road in Blanchardstown. I knew Victor and Cecil Glass. Back then, garages were not tied to an individual petrol supplier, so they sold several petrol brands. Tractamotors are located on that site now.

St. Brigid's Brass & Reed Band is one of the oldest bands in Ireland, having been established in 1826. The name changed in 1970 to the Blanchardstown Brass Band to reflect the all-brass nature of the band. Weekly band practice takes place in the band room adjacent to St. Brigid's church car park in Blanchardstown and the band performs up to thirty times a year at events in the Blanchardstown/Castleknock/Clonsilla areas and other venues around Dublin. Not alone have the band appeared on national television and played on national & local radio, they

Blanchardstown Brass Band in Porterstown in 1934. Courtesy Blanchardstown Brass Band.

also appeared in the final scene of the film *The Purple Taxi*, in 1977, shot on Dun Laoghaire pier. The band plays all types of music and has both male and female players ranging in age from the teens to the eighties, as well as a training band. Our late neighbour, Michael (Mickey) Harford was a long-term member of the band. In 1933, another band, St. Brigid's Pipe Band, was formed locally, with Joe Thewlis of Clonsilla tailoring their tunics and caps. However, this band did not have the same longevity.

Blanchardstown Brass Band – full band in 1959. Courtesy Blanchardstown Brass Band.

The aerial photograph below of Blanchardstown predates James Connolly Memorial Hospital founded in 1955. From the bottom left, you can track the road from Castleknock past the national school on the corner of Beechpark Avenue and on past fields towards Blanchardstown. Granard Bridge over the canal and railway is identifiable. Bradys' farm is before the bridge on the left and beyond the bridge, Manleys' farm (Roselawn House) is almost surrounded by trees. Further on is Blanchardstown village and St. Brigid's Church with its spire. On the right by the canal is a three-storey building, the old flour mill, known as 'the margarine factory,' owned by Crest Foods. Noticeably absent from the photograph are the many housing estates now in existence.

Aerial photograph of Blanchardstown, early 1950s. Photograph accessed in Blanchardstown Library on 26/11/2016. Courtesy Fingal County Libraries.

3.
GLEN STORES, OUR SHOP

This book is centred on our old home in Carpenterstown which is still there, at the junction of the Carpenterstown Road and the Porterstown Road, however, the shop, 'the hut' and adjacent buildings are now demolished.

In the early 1930s, a year or so after he came to live in Carpenterstown, my father opened the shop and called it 'Glen Stores.' The shop was built by Mr. Mooney, a small builder who lived in Porterstown, using tongued-and-grooved timber, faced with galvanised iron. Joe Reid of Diswellstown did the fit-out – he was a talented carpenter and a man of many skills. He custom-built shelving against the outer walls as well as free-standing timber cabinets with glass fronts to display fresh cakes.

Left: Paddy Reynolds with daughter Carmel, outside Glen Stores (the hut is on the right in the background). Courtesy Reynolds Family Private Collection. Right: photograph of typical glass display case. Courtesy Reynolds Family Private Collection.

Before the war, Joe Reid extended the shop using mass concrete. We added an extra storage room behind the shop, which we always called 'the back place.'

In between bringing up children and household chores, my mother ran the shop. Locals were also engaged as shop assistants over the years, including Dolly Hughes, who lived at Knockmaroon's front gate lodge, Eileen Reid, from Diswellstown Cottages, my cousin, Bridie Reynolds, from the Sandpits and another cousin, Peter Reynolds, from Peck's Lane, as well as my older sister, Maureen. Family members had to pitch in too, sometimes amid groans and moans. A knock on the door at dinnertime meant a customer had forgotten something, usually tea or oil for the lamp. This caused rumblings of *'I went the last time'* but in the end, someone had to open up for the customer.

Pretty quickly, the shop served as a nucleus for people in the locality. Not alone did we have a telephone and a radio, but the postbox and the number 80 bus stop were right outside. People not on the bus route cycled as far as the shop, abandoned their bikes behind our hedge for the day, and caught the bus into town. The hut built beside the shop served as a focal point for community gatherings.

Peter Reynolds behind the counter in Glen Stores. Courtesy Reynolds Private Family Collection.

Typical products for sale in our shop. Courtesy of the Little Museum of Dublin.

The shop sold mainly groceries but it also sold bicycle lamps, mouse traps, kerosene and puncture repair kits. We even stocked a variety of fireworks, which were legal back then. Biscuits came loose in large tins with a glass front and were weighed out on request into quarter pound, half pound or one pound bags. Many commodities we stocked are no longer available these days and some food items taste different too. For example, a particular favourite of mine, 'gur' cake, was like a compacted Christmas pudding square with a thin pastry crust top and bottom. Although gur cake is still sold in places today, it is just not the same.

Walnut Whips used to be called Whip Cream Whirls in my time and they came in two varieties. The one with a walnut on top cost tuppence, roughly equivalent to one cent today and the one without a walnut cost one old penny, no equivalent today. Glass jars of sweets and chocolate bars were on display behind the counter. Typically, we stocked jellies, rum and butter, *Liquorice Allsorts, Bulls Eye's, Acid Drops, Peggy's Leg, Nancy Balls, Yorkshire Toffees,* and *Scot's Clan chocolate toffees*, a toffee sweet covered with a sugar coating, expensive but tasty. I also liked *NKM's*, a kind of soft toffee sweet that came in packets of ten and cost a few pence.

Tony Reynolds

Weights used in the shop, mainly for weighing potatoes Courtesy Reynolds Family Private Collection.

When my father sought a licence to sell stamps in the shop, the postmistress in Castleknock village objected, but it was nevertheless granted. He was also instrumental in having a post box inserted into the wall at the top of the Sandpits hill in 1934, which saved many a long walk. After independence, red 'colonial' postboxes with the Royal Insignia inscribed 'Edward Rex' or 'Victoria Regina' and the lion and unicorn emblem were simply painted over in green. These postboxes are still in use throughout Ireland. However, the postbox in the stone wall outside our place was of the post-independence variety – I remember it being installed. Once the requisite licensing had been granted, a notice was erected above the shop which read, *"licensed to sell cigarettes, stamps and snuff."*

Extract 1954 Telephone Directory showing the telephone number for 'Glen Stores.' Photo, Reynolds family Private Collection; Telephone Directory, courtesy the Little Museum of Dublin.

49

Castleknock – Memories of a Neighbourhood

Around 1937, we got a telephone. It was an exciting time for us, watching the telephone poles being erected along the roads. Our phone number was '*Glen Stores 86*.' By the 1970s this had gained a prefix - 383086, then 213086 and more latterly, 8213086. Back then, the telephone was a vital connection for people in the area to receive calls and make calls. The phone was a wooden box with two forks on which the brass telephone sat, quite an ornate affair.

In order to be put through to another telephone, you had to go through the exchange in Castleknock. The Miss Cassidy sisters ran the exchange from the building opposite Myo's pub. They also had a public phone facility, which people paid to use. The phone number for Castleknock Post Office was *Castleknock 1*. To get a line, you had to wind a handle on the right-hand side and it rang in the Castleknock Telephone Exchange. When one of the Miss Cassidys answered, she asked for the number you wanted. Then you hung up and stood beside the phone to await the call. It felt as if you were under a compliment in seeking this service.

Although they lived above the exchange, the Miss Cassidys were reluctant to answer the phone after 10 p.m. and they rarely answered it after midnight. If you got no response (and this was often the case), you had to keep ringing and ringing in the hope they'd answer.

Standard Post & Telegraphs coinbox with hand held phone. (A much later version than ours).

Having a telephone had its downsides as the family were woken from time to time with banging on the door in the middle of the night to use the phone for emergency calls to the doctor or the midwife, or to let relatives know that somebody had taken a 'turn.' As our phone was the only source of communication for people who needed to contact locals, verbal messages were often left with our family to be relayed on.

One night I came home late and everybody was in bed. When I answered the telephone, it was one of the Clarke girls, who was working in England. She wanted me to inform her family in Diswellstown that her sister had been hospitalised in London; she told me she'd hang on until I got back. I left the phone hanging and cycled to Diswellstown cottages. I knocked on the door and ended up bringing Mrs. Clarke back with me to the telephone – her daughter was still hanging on.

We had an ornate brass cash register with a timber base and a marble top. Its high round buttons - not unlike those on a typewriter - had to be depressed to register the cost of each item. It was pounds, shillings and pence at that stage, so the register had halfpenny and farthing buttons as well. At the ring of the till, the total showed in the glass display area, the cash tray opened and the register emitted a receipt for the customer. The reel of receipt paper inside recorded the sales.

Lucan Dairies delivered bottled milk, butter and ice-cream to the shop by van. We got our milk in bottles but in other areas, milk was simply dispensed into the customer's container. Those working on farms attached to big houses used to bring milk home from the dairy in a billy can. Our bread came from Boland's Bakery and Johnson Mooney and O'Brien, who delivered our orders in a horse-drawn van. The delivery men sat up on a ledge in a precarious predicament on top of the van. Dinny Rall was the delivery man for Boland's Bakery for years and Eddie Wade delivered for Johnson Mooney and O'Brien. Generally, they had a delivery boy along to give a hand. A lot of the loaves, such as batch loaves, arrived without wrapping. When these were sold, we wrapped the loaf in brown tissue paper. Customers brought along their own shopping bags, string bags and wicker baskets or sometimes shopping was stored underneath a pram.

The fact that we stocked paraffin was a bit of a bane because invariably, somebody in the area ran out late in the evening and knocked on our door. *'Mammy sent me up for a gallon of paraffin oil.'* Attending to the request involved bringing out a paraffin lamp to open the shop and then going out the back, to where the paraffin was stored - in a special barrel with a sealed top. As you had to use a handle to pump the gallon into the customer's oil can, it meant oily hands when handling the money. After locking up the shop, it was out the back again to wash off the residue in the rain barrel.

Despite having no electricity supply, we sold ice-cream in our shop. A van came each week and delivered what I shall describe as a tin full of ice, covered in insulation about six inches thick. It was essentially an insulated canvas block with ice broken into lumps for food storage. The ice cream arrived in a special container and it lasted for several days. When the ice mass was getting low, we'd phone for a replacement. This fridge of sorts, which we called an 'ice-box,' kept food refrigerated for several days. We also had a 'safe' where we stored rashers and sausages. If this appears antiquated, it might surprise people to know that in the 1800s, gigantic blocks of ice were towed by ships across the Atlantic, and sold off in large blocks. Most grand houses had an 'ice house' on their property, usually located near water, which provided them with an effective method of refrigeration. With the arrival of electricity in the 1930s, we installed a modern fridge.

As most people smoked in those days, we sold various brands of cigarettes from drawers underneath the cash register. *Chesterfield*, *Rothmans* and *Players* brands were considered the very best, in that order. Down the list were *Gold Flake*, followed by *Sweet Afton*, made by Wills and costing a shilling (i.e. twelve pennies equivalent to five cents today) for a packet of ten. They were dearer than *Will's* standard cigarette brands. Players also made a small, cheap cigarette called *Players Weights*, which, like *Woodbines*, were considered more for smokers who were down on their luck. *Craven 'A'* were cheaper than Players and Wills but were not considered a great cigarette. *Kerry Blue* and *Woodbines* came in packets of five and cost 5d. (i.e. two old pennies equivalent to one cent today). The term 'inflation' hadn't been coined and for years, prices never changed. There were no health warnings about damage caused by smoking, nor were there restrictions on where one could smoke. It is hard to imagine now the level of smoke back then in cinemas, on buses and in the workplace. Patients and visitors even smoked in hospitals. My father, Paddy Reynolds, smoked *Players* but nobody else in the family smoked apart from myself. I confined my smoking to evenings after work and gave it up when I married.

During World War II, many foods and various goods were scarce, so they were rationed, which meant they were only available by way of coupons supplied by the Government. Each household with the requisite number of coupons was entitled to their ration of tea, sugar, coffee, rashers and butter. They were obliged to produce their ration book to shop owners when asking for goods such goods.

Types of cigarettes we sold in our shop. Courtesy of the Little Museum of Dublin.

Sometimes having the shop meant our family got more treats than others, especially rashers, which had to be used before they went off. However, this often worked in reverse when customers called in favours and had to be kept happy, which left the family in short supply. For the duration of the war, some items were not available at all, especially types of fruit that could not be grown in Ireland, such as citrus fruits and bananas. Another prized item was ladies nylons.

Potato crisps only came on the market after the war, although they were completely different to today's crisps. Firstly, they were a different shape, more like today's chipsticks and secondly, they came with a tiny cellophane sachet of salt inside.

The shop operated a local newspaper delivery service twice a day within a radius of about three miles. Most people ordered only one daily paper, usually the *Irish Independent* or the *Evening Herald* or later on, the *Evening Press*. The *Evening Mail* was considered more of a 'Protestant' newspaper. My father employed delivery men for this service, including Christy Lawless and Sean Morrison, but family members had to help out periodically.

My uncle, Kit Lovely, tended our garden and McKay's garden on the Lower Road. He also did the Coolmine newspaper run on foot, taking a particular route. His first deliveries were up the Carpenterstown Road and as far as Coolmine railway gate. He then delivered to customers along the canal bank, following the canal path as far as the old school at Clonsilla. One frosty, foggy night in 1937, following a snowfall, Kit never arrived home. My father went out looking for him, going house-to-house following Kit's usual route. When he tracked him to his last delivery point and found out that Kit had never reached the next house, he called the Guards and rousted up a search party. The Guards found Kit's body in the canal, which was frozen at the sides, but not in the middle. They reckoned Kit had misjudged his step in the fog, walked onto the ice and drowned.

When the number 80 bus arrived from town around 6 p.m., a family member was always there to meet it, for the evening's consignment of newspapers. On occasion, I did the evening paper round when I got in from school. Sometimes, small orders of messages like a pound of rashers were delivered to customers along with their newspaper.

As well as the shop and my father's job, we had over an acre of land where we grew fruit and vegetables. We kept some of the crop for the shop and our own consumption and the balance was sold in the market. When customers made purchases, payment was either by cash or *'on the book'* or *'on tick.'* Each item bought was entered by hand into a ledger and the bill was settled at the end of the week. However, times were lean in the 'thirties,' especially during World War II when many families were in dire straits. Some locals borrowed money from my father but not all of them paid him back. One relation from the Strawberry Beds had accidentally set hay on fire in a barn (smoking while courting, I understand). When the farmer sued him, he had no money to pay – my father gave him a loan and he paid it all back. Another good friend of my father's ran a Christmas savings club, which they used to call a 'diddly' club. My father bailed him out when he ran into difficulties and that money was all paid back too. While owning a business in a community where most folk laboured on farms and lived in tied cottages might have had the appearance of affluence, my father also ran into money troubles on occasion, especially when debts accrued with the shop.

When I had bought myself a motorbike at the age of seventeen, my mother was not happy. She worried about accidents and injuries and urged me to buy a car. In the space of a year, I managed to save £220 for a car, a huge sum at the time. When my mother told me that my father needed money to clear the shop's bank bills, I gave her the lot. I used to give up half my wages, so she repaid it by taking less. I saved up £90, which bought me a Vauxhall, a much loved car that travelled the length and breadth of Ireland. There was nothing unusual in people having money troubles as times were hard and wages were low.

The shop did very well initially but with fewer imports and rationing during the war, the shop lost money. For example, cigarettes were in short supply and there was no coffee at all. The odd time, a few oranges found their way to the shop but once the war started, no bananas were seen in Ireland until 1946.

When my mother took a notion and wanted to get rid of something out of the house, like a wardrobe or a mattress, she generally got one of us lads to turf it out the window. Anything for disposal was burned on a bonfire in the garden.

Not alone did the shop consistently lose money during the war but it was still doing badly after the war and never recovered. As my father was never going to be the one to close it, my mother went out to the shop one day in 1948, and simply locked it.

Between 1948 and 1972 the shop remained standing but it was no longer in use, except for grandchildren playing 'shop.' Eventually, my mother got me to clear it out and the shop was dismantled. Surprisingly, when clearing out the place, it proved impossible to sell or even give away the cash register - phone calls to antique shops and rustic pubs like Johnny Foxes and even Ardmore Studios elicited no interest. It took two men to lift it when it eventually left the premises.

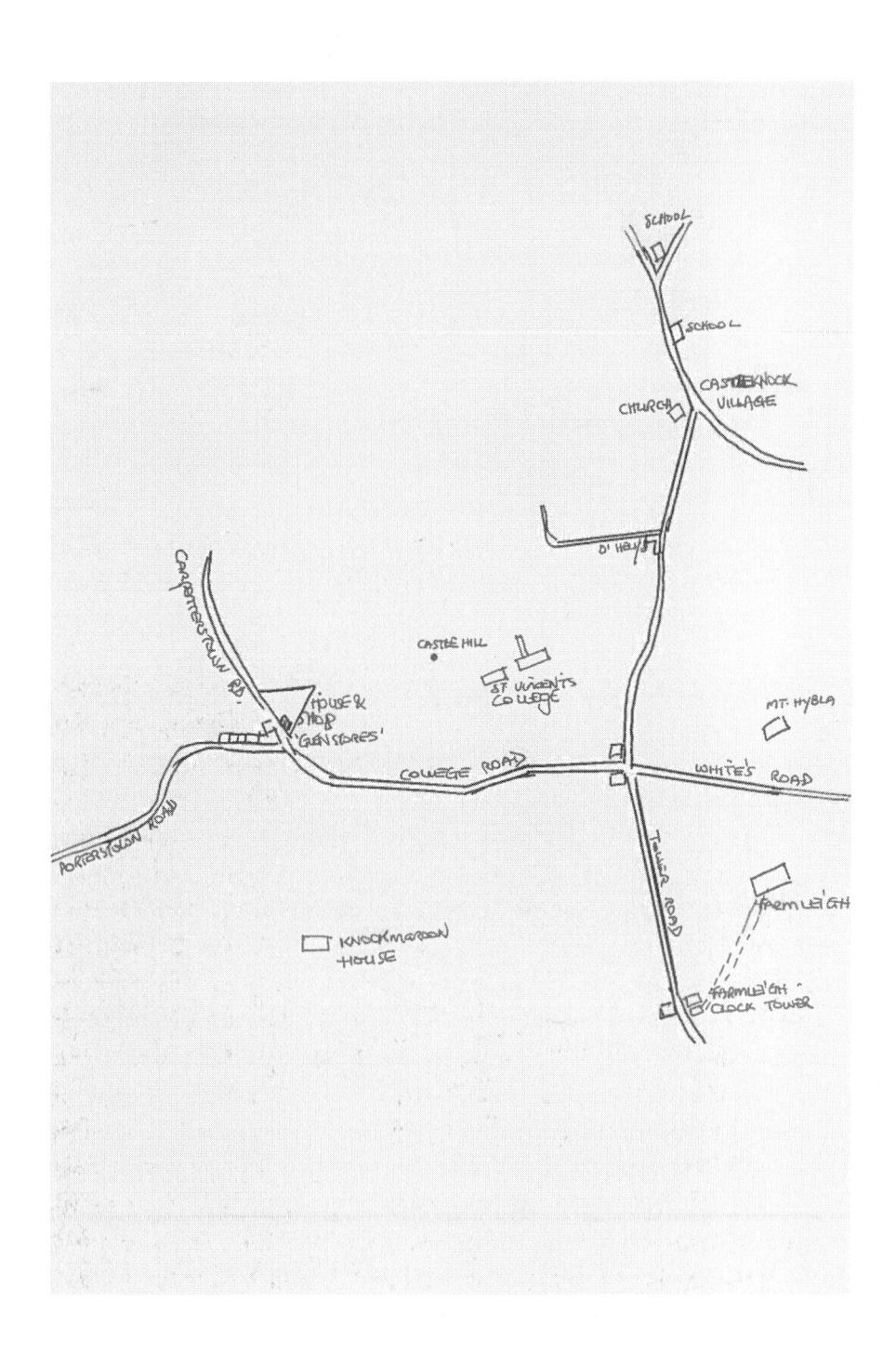

4.
CASTLEKNOCK VILLAGE TO OUR PLACE

Travelling from Myos' pub along the College Road brings you past 'St Brigid's Well,' a principal source of water for Castleknock residents until the arrival of mains water. Covered over with a pump, the well is set within a red brick alcove that borders a stone wall.

'St Brigid's Well,' Castleknock. Courtesy Reynolds Family Private Collection.

Two arched marble tablets in relief bear the following inscriptions from the Bible:

Jesus said whosoever drinketh of this water shall thirst again, but whosoever drinketh of the water that I shall give them shall never thirst again.
John, Chapter 4, Verse 14.

He (Jesus) shall lead them unto living fountains of water and God shall wipe away all the tears of their eyes.
Revelations, Chapter 7, Verse 17.

The huge grey pump was most unusual, standing way higher than the regular green local authority pumps. Although people resorted to this well to cure eye disorders, I do not remember it for this use. Around 1984, the pump over St. Brigid's Well and the surrounding brickwork was entirely dismantled by the local authority who wanted to move it slightly back from the road. Each and every brick was numbered during the dismantling process. They rebuilt the alcove and installed a green pump of the more common variety over the well, which is still there today, although it is broken.

Sheridan's Yard ('Elm Cottage,' Castleknock village). Courtesy Reynolds Family Private Collection.

Originally, the house behind the well was occupied by a Protestant family called Baugh and when they moved out, the Sheridan family lived there. They ran the local taxi service and their place became known locally as 'Sheridan's Yard.' The three sons I knew of were all older than me.

Next is an imposing Georgian house with mature trees in the garden, which backs onto the cemetery of the Protestant church. The two Miss Maguires lived here. Years later, a nurse called Bridie Gargan was living in a flat there at the time she was murdered by Malcolm MacArthur in the Phoenix Park, an incident that shocked the nation.

Former home of the Miss Maguires, Castleknock. Courtesy Reynolds Family Private Collection.

The fields between the Miss Maguires and O'Hely's cottage, were owned by Castleknock College. Initially, three detached houses were built alongside the Miss Maguires' place; Renee O'Connor and Myo O'Donnell lived in two of them. The remainder of this land eventually became College Grove. Across the road, the grounds of Castleknock Lodge ran all the way from Myo's pub along the College Road. Two cul-de-sac estates of detached homes were built on this land - Castleknock Lodge and College Park. At the entrance to the Castleknock Lodge estate, a house behind a stone wall backs onto the College Road. My father told me that at one time, meetings were held in there.

Entrance gates to Castleknock House, off College Road. Courtesy Reynolds Family Private Collection.

Buildings adjacent to Castleknock Lodge, backing on to College Road. Courtesy Reynolds Family Private Collection.

O'Hely's cottage is at the entrance to a cul-de-sac laneway marking the perimeter of Castleknock College grounds; its gable end is to the road. I knew all the O'Hely children. Freddy went to live in Australia. Fergal ('Fergie') was a low-sized fellow but a good handball player who smoked from a young age. The lads used to say to him, *'you're done, you'll die young'* and so it was he got the nickname, *'Done'* O'Hely. Fergie was very intelligent and could outsmart our teacher, Danno, who often called upon him for suggestions when it came to something innovative. '*Perhaps Mr. O'Hely could help us out,*' he'd say, in a sarcastic tone. Fergal also went to live in Australia and did not die young. Maureen remained in the locality. Nuala was in my class at school and remained living in the locality after she married. 'Alfred O'Hely, Farm Lodge,' is recorded in the 1977 Thom's Directory.

O'Hely's cottage, College Road, on the perimeter of Castleknock College. Courtesy Reynolds Family Private Collection.

Towards the bottom of the cul-de-sac laneway, two Protestant ladies – the Miss Newenhams – lived in a two storey house. The ladies were rarely seen out and about but the odd time, the younger Miss Newenham drove her Ford 'Y' model car. It was always in immaculate condition. One time, I spotted it when I was at Glass's garage and took a peep inside – there was even a pull-down blind on the oval back window. 'Lottie Newenham, Farm' is recorded in the 1977 Thom's Directory. I was sorry to hear that the last surviving Miss Newenham was burgled when she lived alone.

Mickey Byrne trained racehorses at a stable yard beside the Miss Newenhams and he lived over the stables. One time when a delivery of fresh eggs arrived into the shop, my father got me to cycle over with a dozen eggs for Mickey. '*Great,*' said Mickey. He proceeded to mash them into the horse feed, shells and all. Later on, a riding school was established in the yard. The sound of whinnying horses in the laneway usually heralded a line of children on ponies heading towards the Phoenix Park.

Stableyard in the cul-de-sac laneway beyond O'Hely's cottage, College Road. Courtesy National Inventory of Architectural Heritage.

An English couple, Mr. Adamson and his wife, lived beyond the Miss Newenhams, at the very end of the laneway. Mr. Adamson was a keen gardener who kept greenhouses, and cultivated flowers to sell in the market. My father was friendly with Mr. Adamson and bought seeds and flowers from him on occasion. In the background of the photograph showing the College's annual gymnastics display, a long greenhouse can be seen near to the cricket pavilion, although it is too close to the O'Hely's cottage to be the Adamsons.

The lane is completely different now – only O'Hely's cottage remains, although it is unoccupied. The other properties that once graced the laneway are gone and that land seems to have been subsumed into the adjacent housing development, Collegewood. The bottom of the lane now curves into a gateway to Castleknock College grounds.

Castleknock College, view from O'Hely's. Castleknock Hill is in the background on the right. Courtesy Reynolds Family Private Collection.

At one time, two cottages adjacent to O'Hely's cottage faced the College Road. The first cottage was occupied by the O'Driscoll family. Lily O'Driscoll was a piano teacher who taught my cousin, Peter Reynolds. A burly man lived on his own in the cottage nearest to the College Lodge.

Beyond these cottages, two disused stone quarries in the College grounds were always full of water. When they froze over, people used to ice skate on the ponds. One winter, the pond was frozen over for a full week and we could slide the full length of it, until the thaw came and it began to crack under foot. There were two concrete buildings - pumping stations - near to the ponds. Water was pumped from here underground and up to the tank on Tower Hill, the mound nearest to the College Lodge, which some refer to as 'Windmill Hill.'

Tower Hill (otherwise known as Windmill Hill), Castleknock College grounds. Courtesy Reynolds Family Private Collection.

At the landmark crossroads, known as 'The College Lodge,' the lodge at the entrance to Knockmaroon, Lord Moyne's estate, was called the 'Front Lodge.' Originally, the Merriman family lived there until the Hughes family moved up from the Sandpits. There were four children in the Hughes family - Dick, Dolly, Dotie and Rosaleen. Dolly worked in our shop at one stage. The Woods family lived there for a time later on.

Knockmaroon Front Gate Lodge, Knockmaroon Estate. Courtesy Reynolds Family Private Collection.

A square granite-cut gate lodge, always known as the 'College Lodge,' is at the main entrance to Castleknock College. Different families lived in the lodge over the years including the Murray family who had two daughters. Jack Murray worked in the College. He was a brother of Jim Murray, a photographer, and his sister, 'Big' Sheila, who lived in the Guinness cottages overlooking the Glen. Jack and his family eventually moved to England and Mr. Smyth, who worked in the College, moved there from the Lower Road. The lodge is still occupied by Mrs. Smyth.

College Lodge, Castleknock College. Courtesy Reynolds Family Private Collection.

Tony Reynolds

St. Vincent's College ('Castleknock College').

St. Vincent's College has been run by the Vincentian Order since 1808 – it was always known locally as 'The College.' All through my childhood and right up to 1987, the college was a boarding school for Catholic boys from well-off families. The campus had rugby pitches, a soccer pitch, a cricket ground with an adjacent pavilion, an athletics and running track, six tennis courts, and stables all set in landscaped gardens, as well as a pavilion style swimming pool, which was still there until the eighties. Many former pupils went on to illustrious careers in politics, law, medicine and business, including President DeValera and Liam Cosgrave. In the 1980s, day pupils were admitted and the boarding school eventually closed. The Vincentian Order was well-known for its generosity to the needy, their kitchen being a regular venue for the homeless who used to walk out from town through the Park and call at the refectory door for leftover food.

Brother Michael from the College was a tall man, known and recognised far beyond the College for his friendly waves. I remember Brother Michael showing me his gun collection which included a point 22 rifle and an old shotgun. One time, when he took a shot from the old gun, the barrel blew up and the shot went everywhere. Brother Michael was over the men and in charge of the gymnasium and the grounds. His office-cum-store was beside the handball alleys, often known as the 'dripping house,' as lard was made in the building behind.

During the summer, after the boys' lockers had been cleared out, Brother

Castleknock College re-union, 1930, showing gym display by the College boys, parents, the cricket pavilion and greenhouses beyond the hedge. Courtesy British Pathe Limited - Film ID 713.17; Still No. 51 (Film footage with no sound can be viewed).

Castleknock College re-union, 1930, showing College boys, parents, the handball alleys and the 'dripping house.' Courtesy British Pathe Limited - Film ID 713:17; Still No. 38 (Film footage with no sound can be viewed).

Michael used to beckon me over. He'd produce a sack full of rugby football boots, footballs, cricket bats and wickets, all left behind by boarders who had finished up for good. He'd give me first pick, often a few pairs of boots, before going on to distribute the remainder to others. Of course, they were rugby boots and I played soccer, but who cared when some of them were brand new. On one occasion, he gave me an entire cricket outfit – three stumps and the cross member to form the wicket, together with cricket bats. That got me playing some cricket alright. Lots of local lads, especially those from Peck's Lane, used to go to the dump at the College to pick up copybooks left behind. Once you got over the smell of rotten grass, there'd be enough copybooks to last the year, with their distinctive dark blue cover and St. Vincent's logo on the front.

Before Brother Michael's time, Brother Pat was a lay brother at the College. He used to frown on local 'kids' taking a short-cut across the college and he often upbraided defaulters with a walking stick, threatening to tell their parents. For us, it was a very real fear, as the college staff were good customers in our shop, as were the pupils, although the shop was officially out of bounds for the pupils.

The College employed ladies in the kitchen who were deaf; they wore uniforms similar to that of a nurse. On occasion, they came to our shop, but they did not leave the College grounds. They crossed the College field and stood inside the boundary wall, waving to catch our attention. Once they had done so, they usually dropped us down a shopping list and waited for us to come out with their provisions.

Brother Darcy was in charge of the buildings' interiors. Although Brother Michael and Brother Darcy were both members of the CYMS in Porterstown, they did not see eye to eye. I often had a game of billiards with Brother Darcy, who was a skilled player, although billiards was considered an old-fashioned game. Brother Darcy used to throw his eyes to Heaven when Brother Michael played, as Brother Michael was not as skilled.

The College ran a full-scale farm so they were virtually self-sufficient. They kept cattle, pigs and sheep and grew their own corn, cereal crops and vegetables, such as cabbage and potatoes. The farmyard at the rear of the College almost backed on to the lane beyond O'Hely's cottage. The College even had its own slaughterhouse. Each week, a butcher came out from Dublin to kill cattle and sheep. Two dairy men used to milk the dairy herd by hand in the fields surrounding the farmyard, using small milking stools.

The College gave employment to locals including some of my own relatives.

Castleknock – Memories of a Neighbourhood

Jim Heffernan and Christy Smith worked in the College for years and lived in rooms at the farmyard. Bartle O'Brien worked in the kitchens at the College at one time. He married Molly Proudfoot from the Clonsilla Road and he later became involved with the Credit Union in Blanchardstown. A cousin of mine, Tommy Reilly, from Peck's Lane, worked in the College. Tommy was the eldest of nine, the other eight being all girls. Tommy was a great man at handball and he often gave me a game in the handball alley at the College in the summer, when the College boys were gone. Other relatives who worked there included the Proudfoot family of Clonsilla. Mick, John, Peter, Joe, Frank and Tony Proudfoot all worked in the College at some stage. The farmyard is now gone. Peter Proudfoot was a great athlete, good at running, swimming and football, but he was also skilled with his hands and made furniture for his home. He drove a van for the College and eventually went to work as a vanman at Shackleton Mills, Lucan. He also did work for other people, including Kevin Browne, who lived on the Rugged Lane. One night I remember being in the Strawberry Hall with my father and Larry Reynolds when we got bad news. Peter Proudfoot had been electrocuted while dismantling a pump in Kevin Browne's garden. I drove them straight to Clonsilla to see their sister Josie, who was married to Peter.

Near to the Proudfoot family home in Clonsilla, the College owned land on which they grazed cattle. The cattle trough was filled with water from a big pump on the land but used to go dry in summer. Some of College men, usually Mick Proudfoot, used to bring water up to Clonsilla by way of horse and cart. They'd fill a puncheon with water – it was a type of wooden barrel on wheels – then they'd hoist the puncheon onto a farm cart and hitch the cart to a horse. Once I spotted this contraption going by, I knew where it was headed and I'd hop onto the back of the cart for the spin. Mick Proudfoot was a nice guy; after I got my tonsils out, he bought me a great toy – a steel boat. You had to fill the boat partly with water and light special candles inside it; once the candles heated the water, steam blew out the back of the boat and it could motor along on a pond.

Castleknock College has two hills of note on its grounds. The hill nearest to the College Lodge, Tower Hill, had a water tank on top. The other hill beyond the College, Castleknock Hill, is a wooded Norman 'motte,' crowned by the remains of an old fortress, now consisting of an ivy-covered tower, and a burial ground for deceased members of the Vincentian Order. The history of Castleknock Hill dates back to the twelfth century and it was once the site of a battle.

Near to our place was the tradesman's entrance to the College, which we called,

Left: view of Castleknock Hill, 2017. Internet. Right: view of ruin and burial ground for deceased members of the Vincentian Order, Castleknock Hill. Courtesy National Inventory of Architectural Heritage.

'the back college gate.' The long avenue up to the College is bounded by railings and a hedge on the right. The grounds on each side were used for grazing, with the land on the left sometimes tilled for crop rotation. Up to the time of the World War II, we watched from behind the railings when the College boys celebrated end of term with a battle re-enactment on the motte, with their parents seated on rows of chairs in the field. When the College team won at sports, a firework display was often held on the Hill. Naturally, we used to hop over the wall and queue with the 'College boys' when they were handing out fireworks.

We always referred to the field immediately adjacent to our place as 'the College field.' We had a path worn across it to the village. One time, I remember a low-flying aircraft took to circling Castleknock College over a two week period, with the pilot performing loop-the-loops and other stunts. Some said it was an ex-College boy - I don't know if that is true. This particular day, the plane kept dipping down near to our chimney and doing its usual stunts, so I got up onto the roof of our shed for a closer look. The plane set off for another loop-the-loop with its nose in the air, when all of a sudden, the engine cut out completely mid-air. The plane fell tail-first through the trees into the College field, bringing boughs and branches down with it. The pilot hopped out of the cockpit but the

Castleknock College, Battle Scene re-enactment on Castleknock Hill. 'College Boy Actors, 1931.' Courtesy British Pathe Limited - Film ID: 809.11; Still No. 15 (Film footage with no sound can be viewed).

passenger was trapped by broken boughs. Gerry Ryan, who worked in the College, ran across and rescued the pilot. Within minutes, the wreckage caught fire and burned to pieces. The charred remains were on the ground for weeks afterwards.

College Road is bounded on one side by Castleknock College, and by the Knockmaroon Estate on the opposite side. The Knockmaroon estate was bought by a member of the Guinness family in 1884 and the family of Lord Moyne have occupied it ever since. The last Lord Moyne who lived at Knockmaroon was married twice. His first wife, Lady Diana Mosley, bore him two sons - Jonathan Guinness, the present Lord Moyne, and the Honourable Desmond Guinness, of Leixlip Castle, who was key to establishing the Irish Georgian Society in 1958. The present occupant of Knockmaroon is the Honourable Kieran Guinness, part of the second family.

Knockmaroon's avenue is lined with tall beech trees that almost join in the middle. The house has views stretching over the Liffey Valley and the Dublin mountains beyond. It is run as a dairy farm but they also keep fowl. In my childhood, Mr. St. John was the steward - we always pronounced this 'Saint-John' although others pronounce it more like 'Sinjon.' Mr. St. John was a man with a military bearing and a small moustache. He had three daughters that I remember.

Knockmaroon House. Courtesy National Inventory of Architectural Heritage.

Sometimes you'd be hacking away at a fallen branch in the Glen, on the perimeter of the Knockmaroon estate, and you'd hear a posh voice from beyond the thick foliage. '*This is private property, you know.*' He never came down to confront us directly. We'd stop sawing, all would go quiet and after a few minutes, we'd resume once we heard him moving away. Daunt Smith was the steward up until the 1980s. The Knockmaroon estate is bounded by Farmleigh, Castleknock College, the Lower Road and The Glen. A lodge in a similar style to the main gate lodge stands on the Tower road, opposite Farmleigh's Clocktower, although that entrance was never used.

Leaving the College crossroads, the boundary of the Knockmaroon Estate

Knockmaroon pasture and dairy herd, 2017. Courtesy Reynolds Family Private Collection.

extends along the entire frontage of Castleknock College. A line of fourteen ash trees stood on the verge outside Knockmaroon's perimeter fence, at a point almost opposite the back entrance gate of the college. The trees were fairly bare at the base, with all the foliage close to the top, a factor which might have lent to the area's renown for ghostly happenings. The County Council cut down these trees for firewood during the war. Needless to say, all the children in the locality went to witness the event. It was supposed to be controlled felling, but I remember one or two crashing into the Knockmaroon side, collapsing the fence. Although the trees are gone over seventy years, this point continues to be known among older locals as 'the fourteen trees.'

The farmyard entrance to Knockmaroon or Guinness's yard, was always known, for some reason, as 'Hardy's gate.' Milk churns were left on a high wooden platform outside Hardy's gate for ease of collection, but that was no longer necessary with the advent of the milk truck. Eventually, the platform was taken down.

A short avenue leads to a Tudor-style block of red-bricked stable buildings. A double height carriageway arch has a clock tower that is capped with a weather vane. The central archway leads into a courtyard. Living accommodation above

Hardy's Gate, Knockmaroon. Courtesy Reynolds Family Private Collection.

the stables in the farmyard was home to many a family over the years. Mostly, it housed those who worked for the Guinnesses including the steward, but sometimes, it accommodated artists or writers or those skilled with their hands, like the late Cathal Gannon, who made harpsichords.

Back out on the College Road and beyond the farmyard entrance to Knockmaroon, the road forks. Clarke's cottage, later Kathleen O'Gorman's, is on the corner of the hill in between the two roads, surrounded by tall pine trees and a hedge. During my childhood, old Mrs. Clarke lived here with her daughters Molly and Kathleen, and her sons Andy, Leo and Eddie. Leo was a DMP man, i.e. the Dublin Metropolitan Police. He married Rose Brennan whose family lived in a cottage at Coolmine railway. They became parents to Tommy, Leo, Marie, Nuala, Tony, Paddy and Olive and they went on to live in the Strawberry Beds. Molly and Kathleen lived on until Kathleen Clarke married Danny O'Gorman, who ran the dairy for Mr. Fottrell on the Coolmine Road. The couple raised twins, Elizabeth and John. Kathleen was the last of the Clarkes to occupy the cottage, which has changed hands and is now much renovated.

Knockmaroon Farmyard. Courtesy National Inventory of Architectural Heritage.

Behind Clarke's cottage, a sharp incline sweeps down towards a gully below. Known locally as 'Clarke's Hill,' the incline is so steep that use of this land is still confined to grazing. Throughout my childhood, 'Clarkes' Hill' was rented from old Mrs. Clarke by Billy Green from Porterstown cottages. Billy was a bachelor who lived with his father and worked for himself - he had a pony and cart and kept a few cattle. He accessed the land through the double gate behind the Sandpits Cottages and grazed his pony and cattle there. The deep undulations on Clarke's Hill bear witness to it having once been quarried, hence the place names 'Sandpits' and 'Sandholes.'

Clarke's cottage. Courtesy Reynolds Family Private Collection.

    The road to the left of Clarke's cottage brings you down the hill past the Sandpits cottages, a whitewashed row of cottages belonging to the Knockmaroon Estate. All the Guinness properties are recognisable as the walls are whitewashed and the paintwork is in a distinctive Guinness shade of blue.

    The road to the right of the fork brings you by our place and then on up the Carpenterstown Road. Just beyond Clarke's cottage, a corrugated tin gate led into a yard with pigsheds. As well as rearing pigs and keeping some cattle, Danny O'Gorman had a truck and did work for the local authority and others who required his service. He also kept a few cattle up in the Phoenix Park during the summer months. When his son, John O'Gorman, married Julie, they built a bungalow on the site of the yard and raised a family there. Beyond the yard, a roadside strip of land belonging to Clarke's was sold and six dormer bungalows were built there, called 'The Sandholes'.

5.
DOMESTIC LIFE

The family hubbub at our home in Carpenterstown was set against the backdrop of the sounds of nature and farmyard sounds - cows and horses, chickens and cockerels and sometimes, geese, as well as the peal of church bells. The cooing of pigeons from Clarkes' tall trees across the road was rivalled by the cawing of crows from high in the Scots pine trees in Guinness's wood and the beech trees in the College field. As the last rays lit the sky each evening, the crows clamoured and took off from the treetops, dispersing and converging again and again until they settled to roost for the night. The noise of the birds was a constant backdrop to the lowing of grazing cattle, the dairy herd at the milking parlour in Guinness's yard, the whinny of passing horses and the barks of neighbouring dogs. Our proximity to the yard meant that we either got the milky smell from the dairy or a smell of slurry. On the odd occasion, a billy goat was put to graze on Dairy Hill, a field opposite Clarke's hill. Depending on the direction of the wind, you could get his strong whiff for about a mile around, hence my dislike of goat's cheese.

The position of the house and the relative isolation of the area brought all sorts of strangers knocking on the door. Most were looking for directions or to use the phone following a puncture or breakdown, which always tended to happen along the College Road. Road traffic accidents were also common enough at our dangerous junction. Many a box of chocolates was delivered to our house in days following such incidents.

One stormy night after the kidnapping of Ben Dunne in 1981, a dishevelled lady knocked at our door. With an awfully polished accent, she looked for directions to Ben Dunne's home in Carpenterstown. She claimed she was a breeder of Palamino ponies and said she wanted to render assistance during the kidnapping crisis. Another night, a distressed young girl knocked. Following a lecture in Mount Sackville, she had got left behind without a lift, took a wrong turn when walking in the direction of Castleknock, and lost her way. We drove her home and enjoyed the box of Milk Tray she dropped in the following week. The College being known for its benevolence, homeless people were regular callers at our house, usually looking for odd jobs, like sharpening knives.

Back in 1939, our house had no electricity and it had no running water until the late 1950s. We did our home exercise and played games either by candlelight or paraffin oil lamp. The days were long and we all had jobs to do but generally in winter, we went to bed early, before the arrival of electricity. I knew families who said the full Rosary together which took ages, but some stuck with a decade or two, with different people in the circle leading each decade.

Electricity meter. Photo courtesy Reynolds Family Private Collection; Meter Courtesy Little Museum of Dublin.

At the centre of the house, our range in the living room was not alone a source of warmth, but it was also used for cooking and heating water. We used well water for consumption and cooking. We collected water for washing and chores in barrels, positioned at the end of our drainpipes. A tin bath had to be filled with water for bathing. When barrel water dried up in the summertime, it meant extra trips to fetch buckets of water. I'd cycle to the open well near Acheson's farm, known as 'Baker's Well', which was down a couple of steps - you scooped water up in your bucket. The odd time there was lime in the water – people used put lime into the well if they discovered a dead rat there – so you'd have to turn back and head for the pump behind the Sandpits cottages. My mother used to wish she was back living in Windsor Terrace, where she'd had both heating and water.

Evenings were peppered with the click of knitting needles, followed by short silences while my mother counted or went back to pick up a dropped stitch. People used to remark on her knitting skills and neat sewing up. She used to knit skirt suits on tiny needles using thready knobbly wool. Back then, people used to get coats 'turned,' which meant the seams were unpicked and the fabric was reversed and sewn up again to give fresh wear. When the coat was worn out, it was often cut down for a child. Another regular act of economy was to cut a worn blanket and sheets down the middle and stitch the side seams together. Although it furthered the life of the blanket, it meant a bumpy ridge underneath the body. My mother used to put clothes into the warm 'side oven' to dry them off. We were customers of the White Swan laundry, who sent a vanman each week to collect shirts and bed linen to be laundered. They delivered them back two or three days later, fully pressed and folded. Another laundry in vogue until the 1980s was the Swastika Laundry, but we didn't use them.

Cobbler's shoe 'last'. A tool to hold shoes for repair. Courtesy Reynolds Family Private Collection.

Meals were cooked on top of the range or in the oven. There was no such thing as vegetarian food or special diets for coeliacs or the lactose intolerant. Vegetables were seasonal and all produce was organic but variety was more limited than today. Jam-making was a seasonal event. During war time, the selection was more or less confined to root vegetables, cabbage, brussel sprouts and marrowfat peas – no frozen peas in those days. On Sundays it was corned beef or a roast cut, usually roast beef, with vegetables and potatoes. Meals during the week consisted of chops, liver, tripe, pig's cheek and cow heel, but rarely chicken as mother didn't care for it, having had an over-abundance of it growing up. In observance of the religious restriction on Catholics to refrain from meat-eating on Fridays, we always ate fish, herring in particular. The dessert selection extended from apple tarts, scones and other home baked treats to strawberries and cream. Much of our family's fare depended on stock in the shop, especially if produce was about to go off. Although our shop had a form of refrigeration in our shop, most people used to place milk, margarine and butter into a bucket of cold water in a shaded corner to keep it fresh. Packaged food and provisions such as rice and tea were generally delivered in bulk and sold loose, measured by weight.

Sometimes a family member arrived home from town with Hafner's sausages that went straight on to the pan no matter what time of the day or night. Every Saturday saw long queues outside Hafner's three shops in Henry Street, George's Street and North Earl Street. The Hafners were an elderly German couple and the story goes that they guarded their sausage recipe and it died with them.

We had a wireless, a rare asset back then. The battery was a square glass bell jar with a steel handle on top for ease of carriage. When the battery needed re-charging, I cycled up to Jimmy Mangan, the bicycle repairer on the Clonsilla Road. It was no mean feat, steering the bike with one hand while holding the cumbersome battery in the other. Jimmy was able to re-charge it as he had electricity from a generator.

Radio reception varied; the longer and higher the aerial, the more stations you could get. Our aerial extended from the apple tree right up to the house so we could even get Rio de Janeiro radio. Mostly, we listened to the national station, Radio Eireann, but we also tuned into BBC and a multiplicity of other radio stations. The wireless was a great source for news and sport updates, the weather and farming programmes. Some programmes ran for years, like *The Archers* which was on at 7.00 p.m. or *The Kennedy's of Castlerosse* or the agony aunt, 'Dear Frankie.' 'Women's Hour' was popular with the ladies and '*Mrs. Dale's Diary*' in the afternoon. A broad range of music was played, from traditional music to classical music to popular music, like Artie Shaw's Band or Glen Miller's Orchestra and crooners like Frank Sinatra and Bing Crosby. They often aired radio plays or opera and I remember Nelson Eddy singing with Jeanette McDonald. During the war, we listened to the overseas Forces programmes and live broadcasts, including those of Lord Haw-Haw, as he was known. "*Germany calling, Germany calling,*" he used to say. After the war, we followed the Nuremberg Trials. A high shelf above the front window housed the radio. It was handy for race days or match days, usually Sundays, when my mother used to open the window and turn up the volume, so the men from the area could gather outside and listen in.

Our garden was close to the road on a triangular site. It was cultivated as a market garden by various people over the years and the produce was brought into the Fruit & Vegetable Market in Mary's Abbey on the back of a bicycle and sold at auction. At one stage, Kit Lovely, my grandmother's brother, worked full time in the garden but every now and then, my father engaged a temporary person to give a hand as well as family members. My father often did the garden after his shift at the Wicklow Hotel and on occasion, George Plunkett from Luttrellstown Castle was employed to tend the strawberries during the season. I remember well the strawberries going off to the fruit market in wooden boxes on the carrier of the bike.

When the shop got busy in the later 1930s, it left no time for the garden, so my father let others cultivate allotments in our garden. My uncle Larry Reynolds, Mr. Drake from the Sandpits and Mr. Sampson, the gateman in the Phoenix Park, had allotments there. Although families back then were relatively self-sufficient and grew their own potatoes, vegetables and fruit bushes, additional crops from the allotments supplemented their own supply. In the main, the garden was used for strawberry growing and to this day, the ground undulates with the old strawberry drills. We also had fruit bushes: raspberry, elderberry and gooseberry bushes and as well, Victoria plum trees, apple trees and crab apple trees. Other crops we grew were sold in the shop - potatoes, carrots, turnips and cabbage.

Around October, we excavated a pit in the ground and lined it with a layer of hay. Having dug up the potatoes and dried them off in the sun, we placed them on top of the bed of hay, covered them with about two or three inches of hay and then covered the lot with a tarpaulin. Once the tarpaulin was held down with rocks, it provided good storage and avoided frost damage. When potatoes became scarce in November and December, we took them out of storage and sold them in the shop. The odd time, rats managed to get into the pit, so it was usual to set rat traps nearby at the time you were 'pitting' your potatoes.

While the shop had been closed since 1948, the 'hut' adjacent to the house still served as a meeting place for the community, and was still being used by the scouts, the band and others, which we didn't mind. By the late 1940s, nobody had any interest in keeping the garden cultivated as it wasn't worthwhile, given the cost of manure and seeds, so our garden became neglected. When beekeepers approached, my father agreed to them setting a few hives. The hives were there for years until the family realised they'd been passed on to other beekeepers. It ended up with all sorts of strangers trooping about the place, so we had to put an end to the beekeeping around 1974.

6.
CASTLEKNOCK NATIONAL SCHOOL

The old St. Brigid's National School I attended had a plaque above the door, '*Scoil Bride 1865*.' It was facing the Castleknock Road and had its gable end to Beechpark Avenue. A small apartment development, Castleknock Court now exists on the site of the old school.

Aerial view of St. Brigid's National School, Castleknock, built 1865. Courtesy St Brigid's National School, Castleknock.

In the 1930s, playschool, pre-school, Montessori and crèches did not exist. Children started national school at the age of four and their first written examination was the Primary Certificate, taken in sixth class.

Castleknock – Memories of a Neighbourhood

Class photo of pupils at St. Brigid's National School, Castleknock, c. 1939. Courtesy Reynolds Family Private Collection. Back row: left to right: Jim Keating, Bobby Clark, Pat Cassidy, Hughie Mooney, Johnny Foran, Tony Reynolds, Josie O'Connor, David Doyle, Tony Caseley, Dick Sullivan, Frank Robinson, Aidan Hoye. Middle row: left to right: Tommy (Tucker) Foran, Pat Hughes, Paddy Spaine, Joe Reynolds, Bernard Ennis, Paddy Rickard, Not known, Mick Doyle, Tommy Purcell, Nobby Daly, Joe Daly, Tommy Clarke, Paddy Gilsenan, Dick Maher. Front row: left to right: Tommy Mooney, William Spaine, Raymond Spaine, Teddy Caseley, Benny Caseley, Tommy Clarke, Willie Doyle, Leo Scally, John Sullivan, Aidan Clarke, Jim Rickard, John Ryan.

Although Father Myles Dungan recorded that Catholic children attended Protestant schools in the parish, this was never the case during my schooldays. In accordance with the religious divide, there were two primary schools in Castleknock, one for Catholics and one for Protestants, both called St. Brigid's. Although they were virtually beside each other, there was no contact at all between them, a set-up which prevailed throughout Ireland. With no opportunity to get to know one another, the culture of not mixing religions created an 'us and them' divide from a young age which engendered a level of mistrust. Castleknock had no secondary school.

Although both boys and girls attended the old school, we were taught separately until the classes were joined when pupils were about age thirteen. After my time inprimary school, it was switched back again to segregated classes. Most

Tony Reynolds

Back row, left to right: (1)Paddy Anderson (2) ? (3) Ray Corcoran, (4) T. Foran (5) ? (6) ?. Second row, left to right: (1) Peter Balfe (2) X McEntee (3) X Stokes (4) X Stokes (5) Marie Clarke (6) ? (7) Jean Anderson (8) Patty Caseley (9) X Maher (10) Leo Clarke. Third row, left to right: (1) Joey Clarke (2) Phyllis (Nuala) Clarke (3 and 4) two sisters (5) X Anderson (6) Stella Clarke (7) Rosemary Spaine (8) Annette Mooney (9) Brendan Doyle (10) Willie Carr. Front row, left to right: (1)Noel Reynolds (2) X Clarke (3) ? (4) Freddie Carr (5) Dolores Reynolds (6) Betty Scally (7) Tina Hunt (8) Joan Madigan (9) ?. Class photo of pupils at St. Brigid's National School, Castleknock, c. 1943 Courtesy Blanchardstown & Castleknock Historical Society. Identification courtesy my sister, Dolores.

children stayed at school until about the age of fourteen. There were four classrooms which held about 30 pupils in each room. Like most schools at the time, utilities were non-existent - no water, no electricity and no heating, apart from an open fire, and of course, 'dry' toilets. Many pupils were children of farmers and farm labourers, obliged to walk considerable distances to school. Some came from Blackhorse Lane, as it was known then, Blanchardstown and Clonsilla. There was no school uniform and some children came to school barefoot.

I remember my first day going to school in 1933 as if it was yesterday, walking past the green postbox built into the College wall at the top of the Sandpits hill. It was a walk of over a mile each way. T.P. O'Reilly, who eventually became a butcher in Blanchardstown, started school on the same day as me. Some of the Achesons of Carpenterstown and Victor and Cecil Glass from Glasses' garage in Blanchardstown started at the Protestant school in Castleknock around the same time. Lots of my cousins went to my school, including Peter and Tommy Reynolds and for a while, the Reillys, all from Peck's Lane.

We sat in pairs on wooden benches that were part of one unit with a seat that flipped up. Mr. O'Leary, from Cork, who was nicknamed 'Danno,' ran the school together with his wife. They lived in Phibsboro and travelled by bus to the school except on the very odd occasion when they arrived by car. Mr. O'Leary was the headmaster and taught the older children while his wife taught the younger ones. From about the age of twelve, they were taught by Mrs. Thornton. When Mr. Allen arrived, he taught the older boys and girls. By the time my own sons started national school in Castleknock, Mr. Allen was the headmaster.

Dan O'Leary and Harry Allen, teachers at St. Brigid's, Castleknock. Courtesy of St Brigid's National School, Castleknock.

Learning Irish was compulsory and it was taught every day. The school day started with a roll-call where the pupils had to answer '*anseo*,' meaning '*here*' or as my son answered phonetically when he started school, '*I'm shook*.' Pupils quickly understood commands in the Irish language, '*suigh sios*' to sit down, or '*line direach*' which meant forming a straight line, usually with two pupils side-by-side, holding hands. The teachers were strict on timekeeping and having homework done.

In winter time an open fire or range was lit in the school room. There were occasions during the war years when the school was expecting a load of turf but when it didn't arrive, the older lads and girls were sent out to gather sticks from the hedges for firewood. The teacher rotated rows of students so everybody got a chance to heat themselves around the open fire at the top of the class. On dark days, pupils were sent home from school early. On a hot summer's day, it was the practice to send two schoolboys with buckets to the pump beside Myo's pub to draw water. On their return, a mug was then attached with string to each bucket for communal drinking water. Lunchtime was always spent out of doors. In winter, some children had flasks of cocoa to warm them up at but some were given billy cans of water that they heated over the fire.

In school, the main aim was to teach pupils how to read and write. School subjects included arithmetic, Irish, English, geography, history and catechism. Anybody who didn't know their catechism got a larruping, especially if they were due to be confirmed. A symbiotic relationship existed between the Catholic Church and the national schools. We were often marched in file to Blanchardstown parish church for functions. The priest paid unscheduled visits and interrupted the class, picking pupils and quizzing them on aspects of catechism while the teacher nervously looked on. The priest used to take a chair into the middle of the room and ask, '*Hands up who was at the May Procession?*' and then, '*Hands up who was **not** at the May Procession?*' Those who admitted to not having attended were told that they should insist on going the next time.

In addition, the priest came on a pre-arranged visit annually to examine the pupils on catechism, to ensure that standards were being upheld. Danno used to become stressed leading up to this event and he'd warn certain pupils, who had the propensity to let him down, to stay away from school on the day of the priest's visit. Coming up to my confirmation, I remember getting quizzed at school and the dread of not knowing the answer if the Bishop asked you a question. The day I made my confirmation, my mother had booked a taxi from Sheridan's to get to Blanchardstown because it was snowing. It snowed so heavily that the Bishop finished up early to let people get home and no questions were asked at all.

When we started back at school each year, Danno used to give us a list of the course books we needed. Pupils learned to write first with chalk and slate before progressing to a fountain pen and ink. The ink was stored in the white china inkwell sunken into a brass receptacle on the top right corner of the wooden school bench. We wrote into blue-lined school copybooks and did our best to avoid blots. Each pupil was expected to write with their right hand even if writing with their left hand came naturally to them. Left-handedness was considered abhorrent, a weakness to be corrected with beatings, until the pupil finally succumbed to writing with their right hand. A term in the Irish language, '*citoeg*,' denotes a left-handed person.

Corporal punishment was rife at school and beatings with a cane were administered for not knowing lessons or sums. Pupils had to come to terms with answering questions and reading aloud, notwithstanding shyness or a stutter. Any engagement or even non-engagement could potentially result in chastisement. A quick lash got a pupil to speed up or to think properly. Fear predominated in the classroom so it was not surprising that school was daunting for kids who had to absorb the strict rules to avoid being slapped on the hands. Slapping was usually with a bamboo cane, which regularly broke on pupils' hands. Even fellows who had chapped hands from labouring or farm work were slapped. The same treatment was meted out to all, although the teachers always seemed harder on the boys. Even Danno was hesitant to slap the girls. Unfairly, teachers often had a 'pick' on those from more vulnerable families who had no champion to protect them.

I remember Danno being hard on the Mooneys who lived up the Carpenterstown Road. Mr. Mooney was a widower and the lads were tough and afraid of nobody. I recall one day in particular when Danno started hitting Hughie Mooney in a fury. Hughie grabbed a brush and ran down into a corner and kept fending Danno off with the brush. Eventually, Danno came to his senses and left Hughie alone. I was sorry to hear that Hughie died only a year after leaving school.

It was usual to learn by heart and we became proficient at chanting maths tables in a sing-song voice - adding, subtraction, multiplication and long division. We had to learn every town along the different railway lines and the parables. Using a map of Ireland, the teacher used to point to an area and pick on somebody, asking about typical crops or places where well-known people were born. One time, the teacher asked one chap who it was lived in Armagh. The answer he was looking for was the Archbishop or the Primate of all-Ireland, but the poor chap was that terrified, he said: '*Men and women, Sir!*'

Sometimes if you got stuck saying a parable, for example, the girls in front would help you out by holding their religious knowledge book behind their back. One fellow asked about Nebuchadnezzar was so concentrated on reading from the book held up in front of him, that when the teacher asked him to spell it, he went on to spell out: N-E-B-U-C-H-A-D-N-E-Z-Z-A-R, not realising he had been sussed.

One girl in my class had this unique habit of kicking up one foot each time she was slapped. Some of the lads took preventative measures when the teacher was out of the class. They used to get Danno's pile of canes and put a tiny split into the end of each cane with a razor blade so it would quickly disintegrate. At one stage, Danno got a strap made of leather, like a truncheon. The lads used a blade to nick some of the threads to limit its life. Danno never seemed to cop there had been tampering with his weapons. Danno was not alone in his reputation for corporal punishment; many pupils left Clonsilla school because of its punishment regime, despite the inconvenience.

Mostly, class time was deadly serious but messing did go on and I remember fellows pulling the girls' long plaits. We had no art lessons and no school tours were arranged. The only formal games arranged were GAA occasional matches in Blanchardstown. Each year, pupils from Castleknock, Clonsilla, Blanchardstown and Mulhuddart attended a sports day. Every few months a library van called to the school. Danno got a few of the older pupils to select books which he kept on shelves so he could sign them out to pupils.

No dentist came to the school but a medical person came and examined all the children. When I was aged seven, a recommendation came from the school medic that I needed my tonsils removed. I remember to this day having to stay overnight in the Children's Hospital, not a pleasant experience, as parents were only allowed to drop off and collect their children.

When I was about fourteen, a newspaper photographer came to the school. Danno sent myself and another few lads off to the hedge at the playing fields with the photographer for a photograph. Two of us had to raise a smaller and lighter fellow onto our shoulders as he posed, his hand mid-reach for blackberries. The next day the photograph appeared in the newspaper.

School ended for most children at the age of fourteen when they were expected to get a job. I finished at national school in 1941.

In 1937, the Government set up a scheme for Officers to attend at national schools around the country to compile a folklore record - The Schools Collection - which is held today at the Folklore Department at UCD. Many of my school companions were interviewed for this record. The records are available on the internet:- www.duchas.ie

In 1960, a new school was built across the road from the old school on Beechpark Avenue. The school has been extended on many occasions since to accommodate the burgeoning population.

7.
OUR PETS

Our family always kept a dog and usually a cat or two and they were often joined by a kid goat who wandered over from Danny O'Gorman's place. In winter, the animals vied with each other to sit beside the range and as soon as we got home from school, we whooshed the animals out of the way and competed ourselves for space nearest the range. The rule was that the cats were put out at night time but the dogs were allowed to stay inside. There was no requirement for your dog to be kept on a lead back then.

Tony Reynolds with mother, Helen Reynolds and Snowball. Courtesy Reynolds Family Private Collection.

Tony Reynolds

When we came to live at Carpenterstown, my grandmother owned a big dark dog. Partial to leftovers from the College kitchen, he had worn a path through a gap in the hedge, down the bank and across the College ditch that divided our garden from the College field. One day when he was missed, I followed his track to look for him and spotted his body down in the ditch. He seemed to have fallen down the bank and broken his neck.

Our next dog was a white bull terrier called '*Snowball*' - somebody at the hotel gave him to my father. Snowball was inclined to stray off for hours or even days and we would have to go looking for him. Sometimes, he would just turn up out of the blue. One day, he disappeared yet again but despite searches and alleged sightings, he was never found. We also had a female Manx cat, with no tail. This cat became vicious when it gave birth to kittens and it even used to attack dogs.

My favourite dog was our Cairn Terrier - '*Trixie*' - that we had for twelve or fourteen years. Trixie had coarse grey hair and he was an amazing dog, more of a 'ratter' than a family pet. He had great senses and was hardy and tough, afraid of nothing. Children from the Sandpits used to be sent up to our house, "*Mammy wants to know would you bring Trixie down, there's a rat under the barrel.*" Trixie used to provoke the rat into making a run for it, to the rat's detriment. I once saw him at Fottrells' kennels having a go at two Irish wolfhounds who lurched away. Another time, I had an amazing experience in a field where stucks of corn were standing upright to dry. Trixie goaded a rat under a stuck of corn but the rat ran towards him, caught him by the nose and wouldn't let go. I intervened by standing on the rat's tail and this got him to release his hold on Trixie's nose but needless to say, the rat did not live. I later learned that Cairn Terriers were bred in the Scottish highlands to kill rats, at a time when shepherds lived in mountain huts. Trixie ate only cornflakes with sugar and warm milk or water.

At night, we'd be sitting around the fire when all of a sudden, Trixie used to hop up and go to the door. He'd sniff and wag his tail and whine to get out. My mother used to say, '*there's Daddy coming*.' When Trixie was let out, he'd shoot off in the direction of Castleknock. Five or ten minutes later, my father used to arrive home and we'd ask him, '*where did Trixie meet you?*' Trixie would have met him at the back College gate or the 'Fourteen Trees,' or sometimes more than a quarter of a mile away, which gives some indication of the dog's acute senses.

Although a great watchdog, he was also a divil for the 'set' he took against some passersby. When pedestrians or cyclists irked him, he gave chase. He died aged fourteen years. When I came home from a trip one time, Trixie didn't come out to meet me. My mother told me Trixie had been at the front door and went out to investigate something on the road. When he was quiet for too long, my mother went out and found him dead on the road, without a mark on him.

A pet cemetery was an alien concept. Like everybody else, we buried our dogs in the garden. The men folk in the family usually dug a hole, in went the animal to be covered over with earth. Our pets are all buried behind the holly tree in the far corner of our garden.

Tony Reynolds with sister, Dolores. Trixie is on the left and on the right is Brandy, Christy Harford's dog, who used to visit our place. Courtesy Reynolds Family Private Collection.

Danny O'Gorman's goat used to graze in our garden and when it had a kid, the kid became a companion to our next dog, a quiet terrier called '*Pip*.' The kid remained nameless, as did the many cats we had over the years. The kid used to follow Pip inside the house. It was constantly being evicted but it always bade its time and sidled in the next time the front door opened. My mother often told me to get rid of the goat but when I went to grab it, it took a massive leap and jumped up on top of the radio which sat on a high shelf. Despite the shiny surface of the radio, it always managed to hang on. Even if I grabbed the kid down, it usually struggled away. It used to make a dash for the high ledge alongside the stairs; it backed into the far corner of the ledge beyond reach, ready to jump again. A few minutes on and the kid was back beside the range, having crept back unseen.

Another time, we found a stray, a curly-haired dog, like a Kerry blue. We called it '*Franco*,' after General Franco's war in Spain, which was newsworthy at the time. We had Franco for a long time but found out that he hated cats. He chased a cat up the plum tree and the poor thing was left grasping on to a weak branch. When my mother responded to a 'lost and found' advertisement in the newspaper, the owner turned up to collect Franco, much to our disappointment. '*Spot*' was another dog we owned.

Another of our mongrels, '*Roma*,' had black curly hair and a penchant for sitting underneath the television table. There was a black mark on the wall where she sat against it. Apparently, she was also fond of chasing the neighbours' children. She only ate Weetabix. During Roma's lifetime, a Cairn Terrier called '*Robbie*' belonging to my sister, Carmel, eventually found a home with my mother. Robbie was a snappy dog who hated the postman. He was finicky about food and only ate a bit of 'rough' liver. Once, when he was being minded and raw liver was dished up, he smelled it and then scraped grass over it with his hind legs. The server later discovered that he only ate cooked liver. Robbie bayed like the Hound of the Baskervilles if my mother left him. One time when she was away for the day, the baying outside the house got so bad that neighbours became concerned my mother was sick inside and they rang around family members to raise the alarm.

Speaking of domestic pets brings me to hens, which virtually everybody kept except us. The Clarkes, who lived opposite us, the Achesons, and the Jacksons all kept hens. The Reillys - my mother's people - always had hens and because they ate a lot of chicken, my mother developed a lifelong aversion to hens and to the taste of chicken.

Another dog that deserves a mention was owned by Frank Proudfoot whose brother was married to my Aunt Josie. Frank worked on the land in Castleknock College and the dog used to run alongside his bicycle and stay with him all day. When the weather turned bad during the course of the day, Frank and the dog walked to the bus stop right beside Myo's pub in Castleknock and got the Clonsilla bus home. On occasions when the dog got left behind, he was well-known for making his way to the same bus stop, hopping on the bus and standing up when he was nearly home, as he knew where to get off.

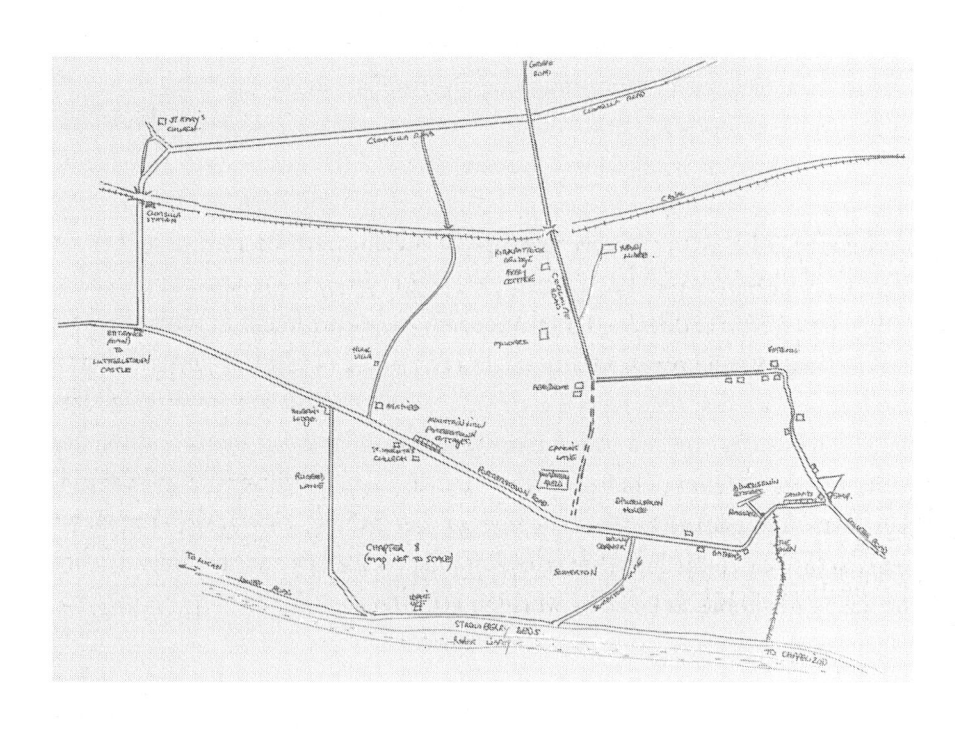

8.
FROM OUR PLACE TO LUTTRELLSTOWN AND THE LUTTRELLTOWN BUS

Two private bus services operated in Castleknock before CIE was formed. Excelsior used single decker green buses which went as far as Luttrellstown but if you missed the Excelsior bus, there was only the Navan bus, which stopped at the far end of Peck's lane. Operated by a bus company called 'IOC,' short for 'Irish Omnibus Company,' the red and white IOC buses were frequent. All buses were single-decker buses back then.

Once Coras Iompar Eireann (CIE) was formed, the area was served for years by the number 80 bus, a single decker, known simply as 'the Luttrellstown bus.' The rattly red bus, with its old-fashioned grey gingham melamine interior, attracted many a stare from people waiting at city centre bus stops, who wondered where it was going. It was a type of 'freak' bus, as that particular model was long since retired on more popular routes. The service was so limited that people knew the bus timetable off by heart and made reference to 'the half eight bus' or 'the ten bus' - essentially, there were ten buses each day. The first bus you could get passed by our house after 8.30 a.m. and made it into the city centre by 9.00 a.m. If you started work any earlier or at any distance from the city centre, you

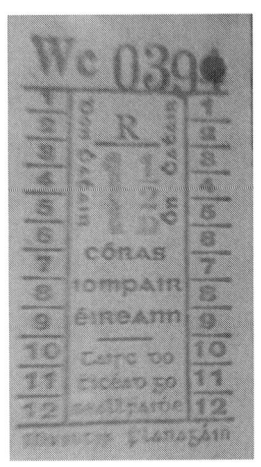

Bus ticket for No. 39 bus. Photo Courtesy Reynolds Family Private Collection; Ticket Courtesy Little Museum of Dublin.

had to hoof it to Castleknock to avail of the number 39 bus from Blanchardstown or catch the rarer number 70 bus from Dunboyne. The same applied to late night buses. After a day's work in town, the number 80 left the quays in the city centre at 5.40 p.m. and with the next bus leaving at 9.40 p.m., anybody living in the area made a valiant effort to be on the 5.40 p.m. bus.

Getting the bus was crucial to getting to work on time so many locals had 'alert' arrangements. My mother used to leave the door open to watch out for the bus going down the hill to Luttrellstown. As soon as she saw the bus going down the Sandpits Hill, or heard its whoosh as it swept downhill, she dialled Smith's phone and let it ring three times to signal that the bus was on its way. Everybody knew it took the bus about fifteen minutes to turn at the terminus at Luttrellstown and come back.

Failure to make the bus home meant a one mile walk from Castleknock which was fine as far as Jack Cruise's house in College Park and even to the College Lodge. From there, it was half a mile in the pitch dark with the trees joining like an overgrown tunnel and a precarious ditch to one side of the footpath. There was no street lighting beyond Castleknock until the 1950s and each side of the road was bordered by wire fences and hedges.

The No. 80 bus to Luttrellstown turned at Myo's pub and travelled along the boundary of Castleknock College, turning right at the College Lodge, then along the College Road and down the steep hill towards Porterstown. From the College Lodge, as far as The Glen beyond the Sandpits, the boundary of the Knockmaroon estate was marked by a wire fence and thin shrubbery.

Standing at the bus stop opposite Guinness's Yard was another matter as the smell of slurry and the milking parlour often wafted across from the

Bus ticket machine. Photo Courtesy Reynolds Family Private Collection; Ticket machine Courtesy Little Museum of Dublin.

yard. The bus stop was directly opposite the wooded area where they put the bull on the cow on occasion. The antics made for interesting conversation while waiting at the bus stop.

Once the bus reached the fork in the road beside our place, it went swiftly down the Sandpits hill. This hill was great for starting a car on a cold morning. Rather than flooding the engine by giving it too much choke (nearly all cars had manual chokes then), it was better to push it over to the top of the hill, then release the handbrake and let the car roll a fair bit down before turning the key and pumping the accelerator to get it going. If a car failed to start on the Sandpits Hill, you were in real trouble. However, if you managed to get it started, the next task was keeping it revved along the Porterstown Road and not letting it cut out, when turning. It was risky trying to turn the car at the Oatlands or Diswellstown entrances as it could cut out and you had nobody to give you a push, so the Woolly Corner near Somerton was a safer bet. Once the car was turned, it was time to zoom away.

A row of eight whitewashed cottages, 'The Sandpits,' line one side of the hill and they abound with colourful flowerboxes in summertime. Built by the Guinness family of Knockmaroon, who still own them, the timberwork is in a distinctive bespoke blue colour. The Sandpits name derives from its promixity to an old quarry. A local authority sign beside the cottages shows the name, *Sandpits Cottages*,' however, they are shown as '*The Sandholes*' on some maps. Confusing, as a nearby row of bungalows on the Carpenterstown Road is now called '*The Sandholes*.'

A pedestrian passageway running behind the cottages affords access to a pump over a well, which was installed by the Guinness's. The occupants always had their own water supply and never needed water from the Ragwell. Beyond the passageway, each cottage has a long narrow back garden that extends up towards 'Clarke's hill.' Most of the Sandpits' tenants at one time were somehow connected to the Guinness properties in the area; they often worked at Knockmaroon estate or at Farmleigh. The cottages have been designated protected structures by Fingal County Council.

I shall do my best to recall the occupants of the cottages in my time. The cottage at the upper end was occupied by Mr. Murray who worked at Farmleigh. In particular, I remember his daughters, Vera and Sheila. Sheila became a music teacher and taught violin and piano. She married Paddy Ratcliffe and they went to live in the Strawberry Beds, later moving to Martin Savage Park at Ashtown. Mrs. Ratcliffe taught my sisters piano while I learned the violin and later on, she taught my own children. Vera lived on in the Sandpits and she always kept a small dog that she doted on, a shih tzu and a dog called 'Dusty.' Not to confuse matters, two ladies called 'Sheila' lived in the locality, distinguishable by the names, 'Sheila Murray' and 'Big' Sheila, latter who lived in Glen Cottages.

Mrs. Bradley, wife of the gatekeeper in the Phoenix Park, once lived in the second cottage but it was later occupied by several other people over the years. More recently, it was enlarged by merger with the first cottage. The passageway is now closed off at the upper end.

Mr. Drake in the third cottage worked at Farmleigh. Together with his wife, they raised three children, Mickey Drake, 'Girlie' Drake and Eva Drake – Eva still lives there with her own family.

A Protestant man, Mr. Sampson, lived with his wife in the fourth cottage down and he worked as a gatekeeper in the Phoenix Park. Their daughter worked in the G.P.O. Every evening, Mrs. Sampson used to walk down the Glen to get messages in Tobin's shop, but she always looked for somebody to accompany her. Young lads kicking ball outside were her usual companions. None of us ever minded going as she usually bought 10 NKM's for her escort.

Originally, my aunt, Agnes Reynolds, lived in the next cottage after she married Mark Keegan and before they emigrated to England. Later on, Jimmy Curry lived there.

The next cottage was occupied by John Fagan – 'Tailor Fagan' – who made riding clothes for the gentry. Members of the gentry often rode up for fittings, trying on garments while seated on a 'horse' model in the back yard. Mr. Fagan used to reminisce about a time when the gentry delivered largesse in the form of a turkey before Christmas. He had eleven sons – I can remember ten – Willie, Johnny, Harry, Joe, Larry, Francie, Anthony, Richie, Barney, Austin, and his one daughter, Mary. The lads used to join their father around the table to finish off tailored garments by hand. Mr. Fagan could no longer speak after he had a stroke; he used to sit on a stone outside the bottom house in the Sandpits and watch the world go by. Johnny and Joe carried on the business. Among others, the Fagans were involved in local theatricals. Mary Fagan made her home there with her husband, Michael Traynor, and their two children, until the 1980s, when they moved to Porterstown. Michael worked in the College. While at Castleknock National School, Mary Fagan, aged 14, made several contributions to the Schools Folklore Collection.

The Hughes family lived in the second last cottage towards the lower end of the row and worked at Lord Moyne's. When they left to take up residence in

Lord Moyne's front lodge, the Bracken family came to live in the cottage. Mr. Bracken worked at Farmleigh. His son, Tommy Bracken, became a renowned poet, known as 'the Bard of Castleknock.' His poetry recorded events in the area and his company was often required for social engagements at Knockmaroon House. After the family were gone, his sister, Katie Bracken, lived on there. At various stages, Katie worked in Bewley's Cafe, in Castleknock College and at Holy Angels, Glenmaroon.

The Jordans used to live in the bottom cottage opposite the entrance to the Glen until they moved to Peck's Lane. Then my uncle, Larry Reynolds, came to live there with his wife, 'big' Winnie, whose maiden name was Drake, and they raised three children there - my cousins - Larry Junior, Bridie and Winnie. Until then, they had lived in a cottage in the Strawberry Beds, rumoured to have been haunted, due to a previous reputed occupant, a man called *Skin-the-Goat* — more about him later. Larry worked as a gardener for Lord Moyne and he also did gardening for others in the area. Most notably, he clipped hedges and kept the garden for the bookmaker in Castleknock, Mr. Molloy. Larry told me that the walled bank area directly across the road from their cottage was once the main entrance to Knockmaroon House. Indeed, the remains of the grand pillars and the stone which filled in the gateway are visible. He said you could trace the old avenue up through Guinness's wood, right up to the house. Old maps show buildings inside the boundary near the site of the old gateway. Larry had been gassed in the war and suffered with chest problems but he nevertheless lived a full life. As for Larry Junior, Bridie and Winnie – Larry Reynolds Junior married another cousin of mine, Ag Reilly, from Peck's Lane – although they were both related to me, they were not related to each other. Both are sadly deceased. Bridie worked in our shop, then in Molloy's bookies; her last job was in Bewley's Café in town. She used to bring us treats from Bewley's when she paid us a visit, an almond ring being a favourite. Bridie died in 1981. 'Young' Winnie married Sean Barron and they made their home in the Sandpits.

The incline behind the Sandpits Cottages was always known as 'Clarkes' Hill' and the opposite bank was known as 'Dairy Hill.' These hills are at the upper reaches of the wooded vale called 'The Glen,' which leads down to the Strawberry Beds, a beauty spot renowned for strawberry growing. There is a steep fall to a stream that runs between the two hills which I heard some refer to as the 'River Dis,' but it had no name in my time.

Across the road from the Sandpits cottages is a right of way path through the Glen. Its banks are richly endowed with carpets of bluebells and the odd cuckoo pint, or Lords and Ladies, as some call them. As winter gives way to early spring, primroses start to appear on the banks of the Glen and young buds on the tips of shrubs. Be it dry and peaceful in daylight, or mucky and pitch dark on a winter's

Photograph of old entrance gate to Knockmaroon (long since walled-in and out of use). Courtesy Reynolds Family Private Collection.

'Dairy' Hill, facing Clarke's Hill, adjacent to Diswellstown and Sandpits cottages. Courtesy Reynolds Family Private Collection.

The Glen. Right-of-way path between Porterstown Road and Lower Road. Courtesy Reynolds Family Private Collection.

night, this pedestrian route is a welcome access as a shortcut to the Lower Road.

A short distance down the Glen, a pair of whitewashed cottages on a hillside - Glen Cottages - come into sight, with their doors and windows painted Guinness blue. Overlooking the Glen, they have a magnificent view of the Liffey Valley across to Palmerstown. Beyond the main entrance lodge at Oatlands, a stepped pathway leads down to these cottages. A Mr. and Mrs. Brannigan used to live in the nearest cottage. Jim Murray and his sister, 'Big' Sheila, lived in the far cottage. Jim was the local photographer, usually engaged for formal occasions such as weddings or christenings. He would arrive by bicycle with his equipment and set up his tripod. Once he was happy with a pose, he ducked his head under a black cloth to take the shot.

"*Will you sing, Jack?*" Sheila used to say to her big black dog. Jack obliged by putting his head in the air and howling out his tune. 'Big' Sheila continued to live in the isolated cottage long after the others had gone and people used to wonder how she stayed on there alone.

Back to the path down the Glen. A wire fence marks the boundary of the

Glen cottages. Guinness cottages overlooking The Glen (these cottages were once clearly visible). Courtesy Reynolds Family Private Collection.

Knockmaroon Estate. Beyond the fence, a steep leafy hill leads up through Guinness's wood to Knockmaroon House. On the other side of the pathway, the bank drops sharply to a trickling stream at the bottom that runs into the River Liffey at the Lower Road.

All the time I was growing up, stepping into the Glen brought the thump, thump, activity of machinery, emanating from the sandpit at the bottom of the Glen. The noise got louder and louder as you got nearer. Then the men came into view, up working on scaffolding and a stilted platform against the cliff face. The conveyor belt was on the go, excavating sand which fell into the smaller holes at the top of the conveyor belt. As the belt moved downwards, the holes got bigger to allow different particle sizes through, until eventually, there were only large stones left. Harris's ran the quarry but it was on land owned by the Lovely family who were paid a sum for every truckload that passed by their house. The sand and stones were used in local building works. The Sandpit gave employment to many in the area including Mr. Carr, from Diswellstown, who was a foreman, also, Jimmy Curry, Mark Keegan and Jimmy Smith, to name a few. Men came from

Blanchardstown and further afield to work there. The year it closed was a devastating blow to all in the area, although by that stage, there was nothing more to excavate.

One winter, this Sandpit was used as a film location. I remember the scaffolding erected along the top bank and filming taking place at night. The cast used to come into the Strawberry Hall late in the evening, mainly for hot drinks, tea and sandwiches. To my recollection, the film was '*Flight of the Doves*,' but I may stand corrected on this point.

On the northern bank of the River Liffey, the Strawberry Beds stretch from the hill at the boundary of the Glenmaroon estate and along the Lower Road towards Lucan, as far as the boundary of Luttrellstown Castle.

Traditionally, the Strawberry Beds attracted Sunday afternoon day trippers, mainly because it was outside the city limits for licensing purposes. Visitors could avail of alcohol here as well as strawberries grown on the upper banks, served in a cabbage leaf with cream. On Sundays, my mother used to warn me not to go down there; she worried about too much traffic. The pubs were packed on Sundays, but that all ended around World War II. The area was also famous for

The former home of the Lovely family at the bottom of The Glen on the Lower Road. Courtesy National Inventory of Architectural Heritage.

its natural beauty; visitors even came from abroad and some settled there.

The Lovely family lived in the house at the bottom of the Glen beside the quarry. Mrs. Lovely was a widow with three children – Essie married Michael Harford, Jim emigrated to England and Jack lived on in the house for his lifetime. Jim used to be the scoutmaster for the area until he joined the army, then Jack became the scoutmaster. Mrs. Lovely's sister, Miss Hoyle, also lived with the family but when she got older, she joined Essie and her family on the Carpenterstown Road. According to Jack, his mother's people - the Hoyles – used to come from England to the Strawberry Beds on holidays and his parents met at a dance in the Strawberry Hall. As well as dances being held there, they used to have dances in the many thatched cottages that once lined the Lower Road, which they called 'house dances.'

As well as frequenting the weir on the River Liffey at the Wren's Nest, kids in the neighbourhood used to collect canes beside the Liffey across the road from where the Homewood family lived. The canes were good for making arrows to play cowboys and Indians and for propping up plants. The designation of the Strawberry Beds as a 'green belt' staved off development in the area for a time. The Lower Road

Extract Telephone Directory showing number for Strawberry Hall - Castleknock 2. Photo Courtesy Reynolds Family Private Collection; Extract 1954 Telephone Directory Courtesy Little Museum of Dublin.

has three pubs - The Anglers Rest at the Knockmaroon end, The Strawberry Hall in the middle, and The Wrens Nest at the far end, nearest to Lucan. 'The Wren' is one of the older pubs in Ireland; it reputedly goes back to 1588 and has been in the family for generations. 'The Anglers' has changed hands several times and is currently part of the Wright group. 'The Strawberry' has always been popular with bikers. My father was a regular in 'The Strawberry' until his death in 1969. When I visited home, we'd often head down there for a pint and a chat.

One night I was in the Strawberry Hall with my father and my Uncle Larry when we heard that my uncle, Jim Reynolds, in Clonsilla, had had a stroke. We

Ragwell, Diswellstown and laneway leading to Diswellstown cottages. Courtesy Reynolds Family Private Collection.

drove over straight away to Orchard Terrace in Clonsilla. My father and Larry went in ahead while I parked. Just as I arrived in, the ambulance men were manoeuvring Jim down the steep stairs. In good spirits, he said to me, *"Ah Hello, Tony, I nearly kicked the bucket that time."* Jim lived for a long time after that.

Back to the upper entrance of The Glen and on towards Porterstown. As the road veers around a bend, the Ragwell comes into view. Once in a sort of cavern, this historic well is marked on a Griffith's Valuation map dating back to about 1848. It was said that on May's Eve, pilgrims decorated a nearby whitethorn bush by lighting it with candles and then walked around the well reciting the Rosary. People believed it to be a 'holy' well that cured sore eyes, especially those who regularly drank the water, applied it to the affected part and took some away. To seek favours, they hung rags on nails inside the well, hence the name Ragwell. This well was once a source of drinking water for locals. An account of the Ragwell's curative powers is contained in Patricia Clarke's contribution to the Schools Record Collection of 1938 - she records the observations of her father, Thomas Clarke of Sandpits, Castleknock who 'knew the well and saw the cures':

There was a well near the Sandpits called the Rag Well. Long ago people with sore eyes came to the well and washed their eyes in the water with a piece of cloth and then hung it up on a bush over the well. When all the pumps in Castleknock went dry it was the only well that had water and the people came with their buckets for water. I am sorry to say it is now a pump.

Clarke, Patricia. *Schools Folklore Collection*, St. Brigid's N.S., Castleknock. Vol. 0790, P.159. Courtesy of Folklore Department, UCD.

At this point, you are in the townland of Diswellstown in the Barony of Castleknock. The Deuswell family, who purchased 578 acres of land from Baron Tyrell in the thirteenth century, gave their name to Diswellstown. Around 1932, the local authority built a row of eight cottages at the top of a steep laneway above the Ragwell. I vaguely remember the cottages being constructed because we used to wander up to the site as kids when the builders were gone home. Each cottage had a long back garden for the cultivation of vegetables and fruit trees. In my day, if you were from Diswellstown, you either lived in one of those eight cottages or on the Diswellstown estate, at the big house - Diswellstown House - in the farmyard, or in the lodge. That was the sum total population of Diswellstown up until the 1980s.

Around 1932, the Board of Health built a wall around the well on two sides with the name 'Ragwell' profiled in relief on one wall. They fixed a pump and a cover over the well to serve as a water supply. The green pump was of a typical style seen around Ireland, operated by a long arm. With the arrival of mains water, the pump fell into disuse and it was eventually removed by the local authority. A metal cover was placed over the well and the site was made into a flowerbed. The carved flagstone is the only thing that marks the site of the Ragwell now. In my time, and we are talking ninety years here, I never saw anybody worshipping there, lighting candles or doing 'rounds,' nor do I recall rags tied to the bushes.

Until the 1980s, the Manning family lived in the first cottage which had a magnificent view of the Glen. Old Mr. Manning worked in the College and Guinness's. His son, Pat Manning, worked in various places including Guinness's, and Clondalkin Paper Mills. Mrs. Manning, used to cook for Lord Moyne at Knockmaroon.

The Clarke family used to live in the second cottage before my sister, Maureen, moved in with her husband, John, and their family. My nephews were keen pigeon fanciers and kept a pigeon cote at the end of the garden.

The Carr family always lived in the next house. Mr. Carr was the foreman in the sandpit at the bottom of the Glen. His daughter, Bridie Carr, lived on there and married Val Convery who worked at building and they raised five children. Martin Convery, who was of an age with my children, was unfortunately killed in a road traffic accident on the Lower Road.

My father was friendly with Mr. Hughes who lived next door, whose children were Pat and Marie. Mr. Hughes worked for the telephone company and drove a small Fiat when few around had a car. I remember him complaining about the size of the car when he stopped to give me a lift, because it was a tight squeeze.

Next came the McGovern family with their children Terry, Georgie, Tony, May, Emma, Chrissie and Detta. Mr. McGovern was a small builder. When Barney Fagan from the Sandpits married Emma McGovern, they moved away before returning to live at the McGovern family home.

Mr. and Mrs. Hogan lived in the next cottage with their family, Paddy, Jamesey, Annie and Gretta. Mr. Hogan worked as a gardener, mostly at Mount Hybla House on White's Road, which is now a nursing home. Mr. Hogan also worked in our garden from time to time. At about the age of fifteen, Paddy left to help out a childless uncle and aunt on a farm down the country. Jamesey often came on hunting forays with me. Jamesey went to England at about the age of eighteen. Annie married a County Council worker. Gretta worked for years in the margarine factory at Ashtown (Crest Foods) and cycled everywhere. She lived alone in the cottage until she passed away in 2010.

In the second last cottage was the Sullivan family – their children were Tom, Pat, Mary, Madge, Dick, John and Angela. Mrs. Sullivan's maiden name was Proudfoot. Mr. Sullivan dressed smartly and had a neat moustache. Dick Sullivan was a pal of mine, although he was older than me, as were his brothers.

The Reid family lived in the last cottage, which is now adjacent to the M50 motorway – Mr. and Mrs. Reid along with their six children including Molly, Joe, Mick and two other lads as well as Eileen Reid, the last employee at our shop, Glen Stores.

Back down the hill towards Diswellstown Cottages and on towards Porterstown. The Doran family lived in the main gate lodge to Oatlands with their children, Luke, Emma and Annie. While the lodge has a single-storey appearance from the front, it is actually two-storey at the back. When I was growing up, water for Oatlands came from a well at the back of the gate lodge. In order to pump, a beam was fixed to a staff protruding from the well and hitched up to a horse.

Main Gate Lodge, Oatlands, Porterstown Road. Courtesy Reynolds Family Private Collection.

Usually urged on by the children, the horse circled the well for up two hours until the job was done. Luke was later employed at the Phoenix Park racecourse. Emma learned the violin - she is pictured in the photograph with her violin class. Annie married Jackie Mooney from Peck's Lane who was a nice guy, tall. Jackie had been in the boy scouts with me and became a painter and decorator. When they married, they moved to Castleknock cottages, opposite the Church of Ireland School in the village. The Cassidy family lived in the gate lodge after the Doran family

Oatlands House. Courtesy Sherry Fitzgerald Estate Agents.

Stables at Oatlands. Courtesy Sherry Fitzgerald Estate Agents.

moved to Lucan.

Mr. Koenig, who owned the Wicklow Hotel, moved from Castlemount opposite Farmleigh Tower, to the big house at Oatlands. Following that, a Mr. Nicholson, a veterinary surgeon, bought Oatlands and he lived there for a number of years. He was a tall, handsome man with a moustache who dressed really well, in horsey style, with gaiters. Mr. Nicholson collapsed and died while he was pushing his car up the hill at the canal bridge at Blanchardstown. Next, the horse trainer, Noel Chance, lived at Oatlands before he moved to England. When the Oatlands estate was bought by the Guinness family of Knockmaroon, it meant they owned the land bordering both sides of the Glen, including Glen Cottages. As a pedestrian thoroughfare, the Glen was always an important right of way and a much-used

Back Gate Lodge, Oatlands, Porterstown Road. Courtesy Reynolds Family Private Collection.

access to the Strawberry Beds. However, it has become overgrown in recent years and fallen trees block the pathway. A vertical post was inserted into the earth at the Sandpits entrance to The Glen.

Another gate lodge at the back entrance to the Oatlands estate on the Porterstown Road was occupied by many people over the years including the Balfe family and Joe Curry, who worked in the railway. The last resident was the late Peggy Hamill, a Labour councillor, who once worked in Roselawn Library. The lodge is now derelict.

The entrance to Diswellstown House is across the road from Oatlands back gate lodge. This large seventeenth century house was bought by the Laidlaw family in the early twentieth century from the Kennans, a Scottish family. Miss Betty

Diswellstown House. Courtesy Reynolds Family Private Collection.

Laidlaw lived there for many years. She was related to Tom Laidlaw of Somerton House. A tall, imposing woman and a lover of dogs and horses, Miss Betty usually dressed in tweeds. There were extensive apple and pear orchards on her land.

A posh Protestant family, the Miss Hamiltons, lived at Diswellstown House at one stage. One of them was an artist of renown, Laetitia Marion Hamilton, whose paintings hang in the National Gallery. I remember her with an easel in the College field painting Castleknock Hill. The distinguished Hamilton sisters, daughters of Lord Holmpatrick, lived at Diswellstown at one stage. You'd hear them approaching from afar because their pack of dogs kicked up a racket. The elder sister was an invalid who travelled around in a basket chair.

There was once a gate lodge to the right of the main entrance to Diswellstown House, where the Chambers family lived. They had one child, Stanley, who was the same age as me, and as both of us had guns, we went hunting together on occasion.

In the 1980s, a haggard about a field away from the gate lodge burnt down. Emelio Cirillo, owner of Nico's restaurant in Dublin, bought Diswellstown House and sold it on to a syndicate who then re-sold it. Much of this land has been built on already and while the rest is undergoing piecemeal development, Diswellstown House, a protected structure, serves as a site office.

The next junction is known as the Woolly corner, so named because it was once a point where sheep were gathered. Crossroads dances were also

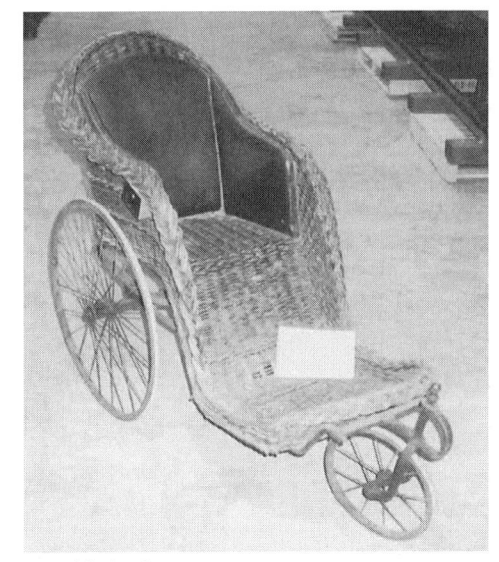

Typical basket chair.

Canon's (Kennan's) Lane – leads past farmyard entrance of Diswellstown House and on to the Coolmine Road. Courtesy Reynolds Family Private Collection.

held at this spot. From here, Somerton Lane leads down past a grand house called 'Somerton.' Once owned by the Brooke family until the early 1900s, Somerton was bought by the Laidlaw family who lived there until the 1980s, when it was sold to the builder, Phil Monahan. The late Mr. Monahan carved off and developed most of the estate lands, including what is now the Somerton scheme, an enclave of 16 houses built in the former grounds, and the Castleknock Hotel and

Castleknock – Memories of a Neighbourhood

Country Club, which abuts the Porterstown Road.

Thom's Directory 1977 shows Somerton Lodge occupied by a William Cooper. The Laidlaw family owned a field across the road from the entrance to Somerton which was used for grazing. When some local men, including some of the Telfords of Porterstown cottages, set up St. Brigid's Harriers, the Laidlaws permitted them to use this field which became known as 'the running field.' The Harriers used it for running and jumping, both for practice and for competitive sporting events. As the priest had no control over this club, another athletic club, St. Mochta's, was set up at his behest. Maxwell Arnott was prevailed upon to accommodate St. Mochta's club on his land but when they needed changing rooms, they were erected out of view of the road, in a hollow at the far side of Mr. Arnott's field.

Opposite the entrance to Somerton, the Doyle family lived in a cottage with an orchard and a unique view over the Liffey Valley. Sheila Doyle, a very sociable lady, worked in the G.P.O. and lived there alone until her death. At a point where Somerton Lane narrows to one car width, there used to be footbridge, once part of a clifftop walkway, the 'Terrace Walk,' which ran a fair length along the cliff edge overlooking the Liffey. Winding further down the hill, you came upon the last remaining thatched cottage occupied by Miss May Tobin. Having been re-thatched in 1987, the cottage burnt down unfortunately after her death. At the bottom of the hill, the lane reaches a junction with the Lower Road. A green pump stands at this point on the Strawberry Beds.

Green pump at the bottom of Somerton Lane, Lower Road. Courtesy Reynolds Family Private Collection.

Back up to the Woolly Corner and continuing on towards Porterstown. The farmyard at Diswellstown House backed onto Canon's Lane, a right of way and shortcut by car between the Porterstown Road and the Coolmine Road. Bordered by hedges of hawthorn, honeysuckle and dog roses, a line of grass ran up the centre of Canon's Lane. In the past few years, a large boulder that had been put in place at the Porterstown Road end of the lane was eventually replaced by a pair of gates that are kept under lock and chain. A pedestrian gate is now the only access.

A field we called 'the windmill field' borders Canon's Lane on the other side. It was a small field so-called because of the huge steel windmill at its centre that pumped water up to Diswellstown House and Somerton. I remember climbing up to the top of the windmill one time, for the view. The windmill field was divided by a hedge from a huge field that stretched virtually as far as Porterstown cottages and across to Coolmine, a size which made it suitable as a grassy runway for light planes. A private aerodrome behind Porterstown cottages was still in existence but never operative in my time, because by then, two larger hangars had been built at the Coolmine end of the field, near the site of the present day Carpenter pub. When the Porterstown aerodrome fell into disuse, the front of it was taken down and it was left open and used as a cattle shed. The odd time, we played impromptu football games in the shed, especially if it was raining.

At one time, fields lined both sides of the road until you reached Porterstown cottages. The Luttrellstown, Annfield, Woodbrook and Farmleigh housing

Cottages at Porterstown. Courtesy Reynolds Family Private Collection.

developments are now built on this land.

The Thom's Directory of 1957 showed the following residents in Porterstown Cottages (12 County Council Cottages):-

Newcombe. J.
Green, W.
Nolan. J.
Gill, J.
Hughes, F.
Kavanagh, Mrs.
Doolan. Miss W.
Telford, J.
Reilly, Mrs.
McDermott, —.
Fagan, F.

Willie and John Nolan were in the CYMS with me and they lived in Porterstown cottages with their father, a retired jockey known as 'Hardy' Nolan. Willie and John were shrewd gamblers who could tell what each player held in their hand throughout any card game. John worked as a bus conductor and followed horseracing, but he was not your regular punter. John and I sometimes cycled to Heuston and got the train to the Curragh. Having studied the form, I'd watch the horses in the parade ring, study the odds and place a bet if I fancied a particular horse to win. On the way home, John sometimes told me he had placed no bets at all, that he'd only gone to the Curragh to watch a particular horse as part of a long-term strategy. He placed trust in the judgment of Joe Manley, a gentleman jockey, and sought him out at the racecourse for tips. Willie worked in the sandpit at the bottom of the Glen before he became an insurance man. Through the Lucky Coady in town, he won a half-share on a horse called Nijinsky for the Irish Hospital Sweepstakes. Rather than having all his eggs in one basket, he sold a half of his half-share to the bookie, Terry Rogers, for about £12,000 and when Nijinsky won the race, he got further benefits. John told me that their father in his dotage took to letting himself out of the house at night and going for a walk. He walked smart and upright on a particular route - up to Castleknock village, across to Blanchardstown, up the Clonsilla Road and home to Porterstown. When the lads missed him, they'd set off in opposite directions along that route until they found him. Willie married; John never married.

Across the road, a house with its gable end right up to the edge of the road had high iron gates. I was always a bit wary going in there because a homeless man had hung himself in a shed opposite the front door. The gates were lately relocated further away and a driveway now leads up to the house. Throughout my childhood, the Buggle family lived there - Mr. Buggle was a bus driver. Later on, Mickey Harford and his wife Essie lived there when they first married. I heard it said that

Former home of the Buggle family, Porterstown Road. Courtesy Reynolds Family Private Collection.

the Hamilton ladies lived there later on, but I am not sure about that.

Next along the road is the GAA pitch; the local club is St. Peregrine's GAA. The priest's house is between the playing fields and Porterstown Chapel, as we always called it. St. Mochta's Chapel in Porterstown is its proper name. The chapel is in the Romanesque style with a cut stone granite façade, a belfry and a spire surmounted by a cross, with a single bell held in place.

Opposite the playing fields, the Balfe family had a farm with a barn and outbuildings. They had two sons. Later on, Frank Proudfoot lived in a cottage on the farm, before it was demolished.

After the Chapel was Lynam's farm, backing onto the Rugged Lane. Opposite the Chapel was Annfield where the Kennan family once lived and where Dr. Troy, Archbishop of Dublin, was born. A road bordering Annfield on one side winds

(A) St. Mochta's Chapel, Porterstown. (B) Annfield House, Porterstown. (C) Entrance to the home of the Lynam family. (D) Outbuildings behind Lynam home, backing onto Rugged Lane, Porterstown. All photographs courtesy Reynolds Family Private Collection.

Tony Reynolds

Hogan's Lodge, Luttrellstown Castle. Courtesy Reynolds Family Private Collection. (Inset) Rear view of Hogan's Lodge, Luttrellstown Castle. Courtesy Reynolds Family Private Collection.

between Porterstown and Clonsilla – this is shown on maps as 'Porterstown Road.'

On the corner of the Rugged Lane, a gate house known as 'Hogan's Lodge' is continuous with the perimeter stone wall of the Luttrellstown demesne. Even in my childhood, this was a crumbling stone building, although it looked more lived-in back then. A sister and brother, Brigid and Paddy Hogan, lived here. Brigid Hogan was the sacristan in the church for years and looked after the altar, the flowers and the priest. Paddy Hogan was about six foot three inches and he worked in Laidlaws. It intrigued people to see Paddy going outside to climb up a ladder to where he slept.

Back then, the Rugged Lane was a mud road with horse tracks and grass down the middle that wound down to the Lower Road. At one stage, families called Browne, Black and White lived on the Rugged Lane. Another house was biblically named 'Pilgrim's Land,' but it was only because Joe Pilgrim lived there. I knew Kevin Browne and his wife, Josie. Peter Melia lived in a pretty cottage at the very bottom of Rugged Lane until he died.

Back up the Rugged Lane and following the wall of the Luttrellstown demesne in the direction of Lucan, a Mr. Casey, an accountant, had a house on the opposite side of the road. He owned several dogs we 'borrowed' from time to time. A gateway led into the yard at the back of Casey's house. Casey's was bought by the Molloys of Liquor Store fame. Beyond Casey's there were two cottages, one of which was

Castleknock – Memories of a Neighbourhood

Rugged Lane, view from Porterstown Road end. Courtesy Reynolds Family Private Collection.

occupied by the Plunkett family.

Next was a large house on an estate owned by Mrs. Kavanagh who ran a city centre business; she lived there with her two daughters. She used to attend Mass at Porterstown Chapel dressed to the nines and they'd go straight up to the top of the chapel, the mother looking as young as the daughters. I knew Parky Ludlow who lived with his parents in the gate lodge at Kavanagh's.

The majestic entrance gates into Luttrellstown Castle are at the junction of the Luttrellstown Road, where the road sweeps around the corner from Clonsilla.

Luttrellstown Castle. Courtesy Old Historic Photos.

This was always used as the entrance to the castle – the 'Grand Lodge' entrance on the Lower Road was never used in my time. Luttrellstown Castle is a walled-in demesne of 600 acres with history stretching back to about the twelfth century. Queen Victoria visited the estate twice during her reign, in 1849 and in 1900. Her 1900 visit was commemorated by the erection of an obelisk near the waterfall on the estate, where she had taken tea. Her visit was more irreverently recorded in the lines of the well-known song: *"The Queen she came to call on us, She wanted to see all of us, Good job she didn't fall on us, She's eighteen stone."* The estate overlooks the Liffey Valley with views stretching to the wooded banks of the river and the fine greens of the Hermitage at Ballydowd in Lucan. At one stage, the name of the estate changed to 'Woodlands,' which appears on some maps, but the name later reverted to Luttrellstown Castle. In the 1930s, the estate was gifted by Ernest Arthur Guinness to his daughter, the Honourable Aileen Guinness, one of the 'Golden Guinness Girls.' She invited many illustrious guests over the years, including Hollywood stars like Douglas Fairbanks Junior and in later times, Prince Rainier and Princess Grace of Monaco.

Before World War II, whenever a plane went overhead, us kids knew it was going to the airfield used by the Guinness family at Coolmine and so we'd race up there to watch the action. Sometimes, you'd spot a chauffeur-driven limousine swishing down the Sandpits Hill and on towards Porterstown. Of course, that all stopped with the arrival of war. After the war, the aircraft hangars lay idle.

The Luttrellstown estate was let to the Italian ambassador for some years until he took up residence in Lucan. It was virtually abandoned during the war years so we were inclined to use it as another public park until the chatelaine arrived back and 'no trespassing' notices were erected by the new steward. After the war, local gossip had it that Aileen Guinness flew on a Tuesday from Dublin Airport to Paris to have her hair done and flew back home in time to host a dinner party on Thursday.

In 1953, Luttrellstown was used as the film location for *'Knights of the Round Table,'* starring Robert Taylor and Ava Gardner. A gang of kids plagued the film set, hiding behind walls and hedges, anxious not to miss the goings on. After the crew left each day, they hunted for souvenirs. My brother, Noel, collected arrows from the film set and they were at home for years. In the 1970s, when the contents of Luttrellstown Castle went up for auction, the catalogue cost IR£25, an exorbitant sum, probably so-priced to attract only serious bidders, rather than the hoi polloi. The newspapers were full of descriptions of the lots, which included linen that had never been removed from its wrappers, some of it moth-eaten. The demesne was bought over by a consortium who developed it into the Luttrellstown Hotel and Golf resort. The castle hosted the wedding of David and Victoria Beckham.

Beyond the main entrance to Luttrellstown is Beech Park, former home of Jonathan and Daphne Shackleton, descendants of the famous explorer, Ernest Shackleton. Beech Park's walled garden became renowned for its alpine and herbaceous plants. The Shackletons had another property along the Lower Road, Anna Liffey Mills, also known as the Devil's Mill, which gave employment in the area. Over the years, many different people lived in the gate lodge at Beech Park,

Courtyard, Beech Park House, formerly owned by the Shackleton family. Courtesy Reynolds Family Private Collection.

including Joe Fagan.

During my childhood, there were no houses at all between Beech Park and the high bridge at Barberstown. At the railway bridge, a gateman's lodge stood opposite a large house where the Clenaghan family lived. Thom's Directory 1942 records 'Hugh Clenaghan, Barberstown, Farm. £217.10.' The son of the house, who was in his early 20s, had the best pony and trap in the locality. He used to come flying around the corner at the Ragwell and up Sandpits hill. Beyond the railway, there were four two-storey council cottages; Tommy Plunkett worked for the Council and lived in one of those cottages.

9.
EXTRA-CURRICULAR ACTIVITIES

Growing up in the heart of a rural community within striking distance of the city had its advantages - children developed a familiarity with all aspects of farming as well as having access to urban activities. The area afforded a measure of freedom as well as a vast range of indoor, outdoor, formal and informal pursuits, although we spent as much time as possible out of doors.

    We lived within the cycles of farm life, surrounded by cultivated fields, planted with all types of crops including wheat, barley, corn and other cereal crops. Accustomed to watching farmers furrow, sow and reap, we were often called on to assist at harvest time. Weather and its effects were a constant topic of discussion and children were attuned to climate. It was commonplace, especially for lads, to wander freely through the fields unrestrained by parents who were probably glad to have them out from under their feet. We plodded about alone or with pals, following in the tracks of birds and rabbits, dogs and foxes. We dawdled or waded or fished in the Liffey and the Royal Canal, only arriving home in time for meals. We acquired a knowledge of where best to shelter from rain, the best places for shooting and fishing and how to make mischief. There were few scruples then about killing wild animals, much less tricking neighbours. Our only concern was getting into trouble ourselves.

    One of the tricks we played on unwitting cyclists or pedestrians was 'the parcel game.' We'd get a shoe box and wrap it nicely in brown paper and firmly attach some cat gut fishing line to it. We'd choose a good spot on the road to put the parcel and extend the cat gut line in behind a hedge or a hole in a wall nearby. A

Favourite venue for 'parcel' game – opposite the Ragwell, Porterstown Road, Diswellstown. Courtesy Reynolds Family Private Collection.

favourite place was the hole at the bottom of the wall directly opposite the Ragwell, which is still there. Another hiding place was behind a bush on College Road. By the time we had it all set up, we'd usually have gathered a few onlookers. We'd all hide, watching and waiting for an unsuspecting cyclist to come along and we'd start tittering as the victim got nearer. Without exception, the next cyclist dismounted as soon as they spotted the parcel. At the very minute they went to pick it up, we'd give a small tug and pull it away. They'd reach further and find it tugged away just a little again and again until they realised there was a trick afoot. Some were annoyed at being tricked and started muttering abuse, while others hopped on their bicycles and rode off, embarrassed.

Paper chases were popular too. One person set off and laid a paper trail to be followed by others on foot. In later years, the area was popular for treasure hunts by car, with many an eager passenger knocking on our door with clues to be solved. Clues often involved local place names, such as Sunday's Well, a house owned by Mr. Fottrell which once stood on the corner of the College Gate estate, or reference to the sale of apples by the Chatterton family, or Flintstones, the name of a house near to the Castleknock gate of the Phoenix Park.

Some kids were known locally as tricksters. One tall chap from Peck's Lane who wore glasses, a few years ahead of me at school, got up to all sorts of tricks. He later won medals in running at Santry Stadium. On the other hand, certain individuals were more prone than others to having tricks played upon them. One man who used to come into our shop was known to enjoy a few pints on his way home from work on a Friday evening. While he was inside the shop, somebody tied a string from his saddle to a post in the hedge so that every time he tried to ride away, he was pulled back.

Another time, they lifted his saddle and put it back to front and when he rode away, you could see by the expression on his face that he knew something wasn't right but nevertheless, he kept on cycling. He dismounted soon after and kept looking at his bike but with a few drinks on him, could not figure out what was wrong. Another time, kids got a type of firework called a *squib* - another name for it was a *boy scout rouser* – and lit the fuse just before the poor cyclist mounted his bike. Before he'd even reached the corner, the firework emitted a tremendous bang.

Fishing was another pastime. Netting for pinkeens progressed to rod fishing for perch, pike and eels in the Royal Canal, although we never ate them as the canal was a bit murky. Sometimes we tried our luck catching salmon, trout or pike in the Liffey. One day near the Wren's Nest, we came across a huge salmon caught in a pool but when we turned it over, it was infested with lice. It was a 'spent' salmon, returning downstream having spawned. We looked out for wildlife, foxes' dens and birds' nests; we could readily identify a species from the eggs.

Keeping pigeons was another hobby. I started off with just a pair, male and female. Having mated four times in a season and brought home others on their travels, I ended up with twenty-five pigeons. To get them to race successfully, you had to separate males from females for some days before a race. I'd arrange for the males to race from a distant point, often Liverpool – they'd fly home quick enough to the females.

Clarke's field was popular for playing cowboys and Indians. Naturally, everybody wanted to be a cowboy as they were always perceived the winners; we had been conditioned by *Hopalong Cassidy* and other screen characters. Other games we played were darts, marbles, pitch and toss, relievo. Team sports we played included badminton, football, table tennis and darts. In Autumn, we collected chestnuts, hardened them by the fire, skewered a hole and threaded a string through it to make a 'conker.' Opponents went head-to-head and bashed their conkers against one another until one smashed. The owner of the surviving conker won.

Castleknock – Memories of a Neighbourhood

Reading was another pastime - girls' comics that I remember are the *Bunty* and *Judy*; boys' comics included the *Beano, Dandy, Topper, Beezer, Rover, Knockout, Wizard* and *Hotspur*. Needless to say, I got a peek at them in the shop. There were boys' books too, such as the *Champion, Magnet, Gem, Film Fun, Adventure*, also, *Billy Bunter* stories. As well as newspapers, adults enjoyed the *Ireland's Own, The Reader's Digest* and the *Freeman's Journal*.

Handball was more of a lads' pastime that we played at the handball alleys in Castleknock College, more so over the summer, when the College boys were gone. Peter Proudfoot, Andy Hill, Bartle O'Brien, Benny O'Connor and myself were into handball. As we got older, another hobby was tinkering with motor bikes and cars.

Music was a pursuit for those who could afford lessons. The Reynolds family were known to be musical. In 1914, before my time, a brother of my mother's, Philip Reilly, played 'drums' in the army band. My uncle Peter Reynolds played an instrument in the Colmcille Ceili band which was often on the radio. On Sunday nights, he played at Ceilis in the Mansion House, for which he earned the princely sum of 25 shillings – afterwards, he cycled home across the Phoenix Park. My cousin, also Peter Reynolds, was the organist in Blanchardstown Church for over forty years, for which service he was rewarded with a medal from Rome on his retirement in 2015. Peter learned to play piano with Lily O'Driscoll. Another local music teacher, Mrs. (Sheila) Ratcliffe, taught violin and piano. Mrs. Ratcliffe taught my sisters, Carmel and Dolores, piano and they became very proficient. She taught me violin but although I gained a certificate at 86% standard, I disliked the violin. My brother, Noel, and sister, Carmel, also went to violin lessons; Carmel went on to play in a band run by Mrs. Ratcliffe. I also played the harmonica with the Scouts band, although it was inclined to cause chapped lips. The photo shows local musicians with their violins.

A spinner or 'topper', sitting on top of school desk, old inkwell visible. Courtesy Reynolds Family Private Collection.

Tony Reynolds

Mrs. Sheila Ratcliffe's violin class. Courtesy Reynolds Private Family Collection. Back row, left to right: Kathleen Reynolds (cousin), Frances McEntee, (?), (?), (?), (?), Sadie Reilly (cousin), Sheila Murray. Middle row, left to right: Carmel Reynolds, (sister), Rita Purcell, Chrissie McGovern, Sheila Byrne, Emmy Doran, Betty Gill, Patty Clarke, Chrissie Brady, (?). Bottom row, left to right: Tommy Byrne, Jim Byrne, (?), (?), Pat Hughes, (?).

Photograph of the running club. Courtesy Reynolds Private Family Collection. Back row, left to right: Joe Reid, Pat Sullivan, ? Mr. Carter, (a soldier at McKee Barracks?), X Telford, Frankie Hughes, Unknown, Unknown, Andy Hill, X Mooney, Joe Carr, Danny Rogers, J. ('Hair Oil') Nolan. Front row, left to right: Christy Morrison, Unknown, Raphie Byrne, Vincent Sheridan, Kit Mooney, Unknown, Jimmy Smith, Unknown.

St. Mochta's A.F.C. Back row, left to right: Paddy O'Leary, P. Lynch, Larry Reynolds, Peter Proudfoot, K. Kelly, Jimmy Keating, Lawrence Keane, Gerry Sharpe. Front row, left to right: John Nolan, B. Keating, Joe Reynolds, G. English, Peter Balfe, J. Balfe, Dan Manning.

Apart from games for fun and sports, we engaged in other pursuits. We used to go mushroom picking in the season, usually around the end of August. Although the College field beside us had mushrooms, the best mushroom field in the area was Daisy Hill, opposite Clarke's Hill. Laidlaws' fields were also plentiful. Early morning was best for mushroom picking, the earlier the better, as the neighbours would be out there too. My mother used to cook the mushrooms in milk; others fried them on a pan of butter. We also picked blackberries in Autumn which my mother used for jam-making. As we got older, some of us worked for local farmers, hoeing mangolds or picking turnips, strawberries or dropped potatoes.

As soon as we heard the noise of the threshing machines at Diswellstown, we'd head up there to investigate. The reeks were thrown to the top of the threshing machine where their binding was cut and they were dropped into the drum. The grain came out at one end of the thresher and into sacks, the straw came out the other end and the chaff was left in the middle. One person was busy removing sacks, replacing them with empty sacks while another person removed the straw and formed it into reeks. Despite dire warnings, we could not resist jumping into the "chaff" coming out of the chute.

We used to hitch a ride on the empty bogies from the College that were headed for their fields in Clonsilla to collect haycocks, although there was no room for passengers on the way back as they loaded them to full capacity.

We played in the wood across the road, Lord Moyne's wood, we called it. We fled when the steward appeared, but once he was out of sight, we were back again.

A memorable adventure was the year of the massive snowfall around 1932, when I was aged five. There was nothing but a bank of snow when we opened the front door and you could only see the tops of the trees. We were marooned for a few days and my father couldn't go to work, an extraordinary event. My father dug a passageway out to the road. Mr. Fottrell got his workers to dig down from his house so his milk float could get through. We happily traversed the pathways amid the banks of snow until it started to melt. I remember playing in the snow by the gooseberry bushes in the back garden when a mound of snow caved underneath me. My sister Maureen had to haul me out of the snowdrift. Eventually, the Luttrellstown bus made it down the College Road, thus ending our foray.

I also recall the 'Big Snow' in May of 1947, the coldest and harshest winter in living memory. When the leaves were on the trees, a snowfall caused large boughs to break off the horse chestnut trees in front of the College. In the 1970s, a storm caused twelve trees to fall along the College Road, a spectacle which my own children enjoyed. The heaviest fall I recall in recent years was a blizzard in January 1982 which painted Ireland white for the best part of three weeks. News bulletins reported on the hundreds of motorists that had to be rescued from their cars of people stranded in various places, including the airports. It was a bonanza for my children who were ideally located for tobogganing on all sort of improvised sleighs and fertilizer bags down the Sandpits Hill.

Growing up, I never remember a circus in Castleknock but I do remember the odd circus coming to Carroll's field behind the Greyhound Pub in Blanchardstown, which was also the local sports field. In the 1990s, the circus came to the College field, adjacent to our place. It was amazing to fall asleep to the roar of an elephant or squabbling monkeys. We noticed the elephants never made for the foliage on the trees but instead, tried constantly to raid the truck where their feed was kept, succeeding on several occasions to unearth a sack of food. Monkeys swung on the trees above the ditch dividing our place from the College field. Once, they went crazy when we were outside eating corn-on-the-cob – we reckoned they thought we were eating bananas. We threw a banana to one monkey who caught it and started peeling the skin bit by bit before scoffing it. Strangely enough, before the arrival of the circus, my wife had this recurrent dream of going out the back in the dark and coming face to face with a lion that had escaped from the Zoo – luckily it never came to pass!

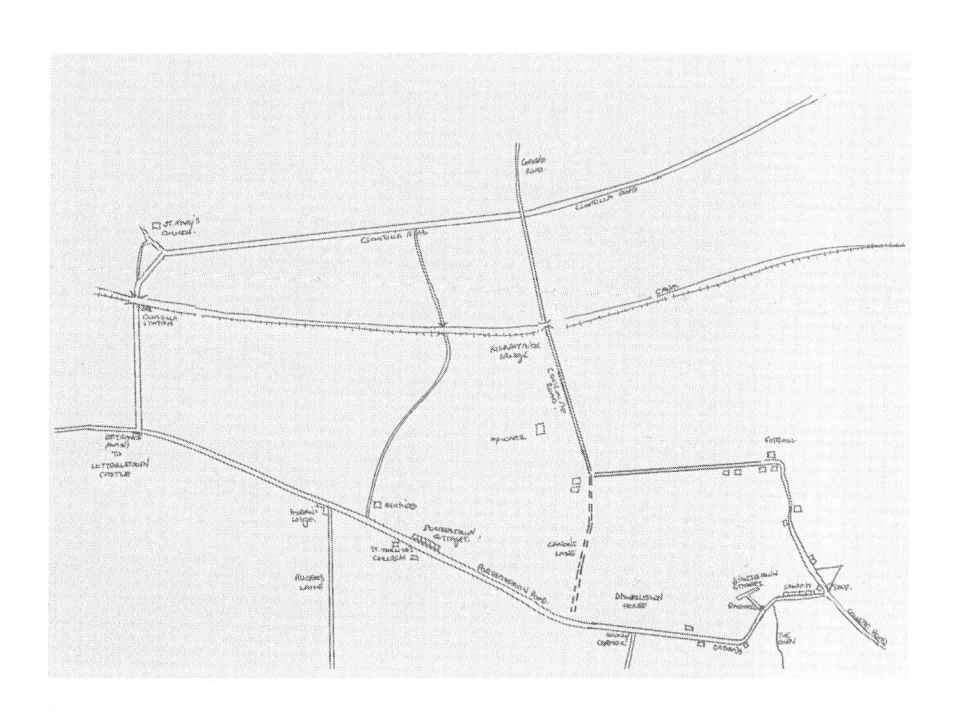

10.
THE COOLMINE ROAD NEWSPAPER RUN

The Coolmine run involved deliveries to customers up along the Carpenterstown Road, Coolmine, Clonsilla, across the railway track down to Porterstown and then on home.

A pair of semi-detached cottages next door to us on the Carpenterstown Road had long gardens for growing fruit and vegetables. Old Mrs. Harford, her daughter, Kathleen, and Christy Harford lived in the first cottage, with their dog, Brandy. I remember walking by my mother's side, holding onto the pram when she visited old Mrs. Harford. Although she was bedridden, the bedlinen was always immaculate. Christy worked as an insurance man and went around on a bicycle until he got a Ford van. The odd time, he'd call to see if I was free to go for a spin. One time, we cycled as far as the Hell Fire Club, where he had business with people living in a yard at the bottom. Christy gave me a drive in the van when I was about sixteen. There was no such thing as formal driving lessons or driver testing; many learned to drive up the Phoenix Park. You simply bought a driving licence over the counter without any requirement to pass a driving test, much less a theory test. My abiding memory inside Christy's house is the scorch marks around the edge of the oblong table where Christy had left cigarettes burning and then gone off to do something. Christy was on his own at that stage and he lived on there until he died.

Michael (Mickey) Harford and his wife, Essie, a sister of Jack Lovely, later made their home there. Having joined the Irish Army, Mickey later became a draughtsman in the Ordnance Survey. He remained a stalwart on the community

Mr. Jackson with Dolores Reynolds. Courtesy Reynolds Family Private Collection.

and church fronts until his death. He had long service with the Blanchardstown Brass Band, as have some of his sons. The family dog, Nelson, caused confusion one time. The dog followed our local G.P., Dr. Nelson, down the path when he went outside following a home visit. *"Nelson, come back here!"* Mickey shouted after the dog.

Mr. and Mrs. Jackson lived in the adjoining cottage, which was supplied by the County Council, where Mr. Jackson worked. They were a childless couple. Their kitchen table had wire wrapped around its legs and they kept chickens inside this 'pen.' My mother often called up with scraps of food for the hens. Mr. Jackson used to sit at his fireplace smoking his pipe. Sometimes, he walked slowly down to our place, puffed by the time he got down, then he'd sit smoking by our fire.

Mrs. Jackson used to bring produce into the market on the back of a horse and cart. After a few drinks at the 'early hours' pubs in Smithfield Market, she'd set off for home but promptly fall asleep on the cart. The horse used to find its own way home and come to a stop at Jackson's gate. A niece of the Jacksons, Betty Gill, came to live with the Jacksons. She married Jimmy Smith from Blanchardstown, who worked for the Council. They lived in the cottage for the rest of their lives and raised five children. Betty was a renowned ballroom dancer who won many prizes in her time.

The homes of the Smith and Harford families. Courtesy Reynolds Family Private Collection.

The College grew wheat and barley in the fields beyond Smith's cottage, which my mother always referred to as 'Captain Steed's fields.' As a Captain Steed lived at Clonsilla House until the 1920s, perhaps he owned or rented land here. These fields were home to corncrakes, which have now almost died out in Ireland. From our house, you could hear their distinctive craking all night long. Collegefort is now built on that land.

Right opposite the cottages, Kathleen O'Gorman owned the strip of land which now houses a row of detached dormer bungalows, The Sandholes. Beyond this strip is a maze of tunnels, created by brambles, all the way down Clarke's Hill to the gully at the bottom.

Steps along here led down to a water source known as 'Baker's Well.' Achesons' farm was next to the well – there were two girls and five boys in the Acheson family. The Achesons ran their farm in an old fashioned way; they reared cattle and kept one or two cows for milk and butter-making and like most people, they kept hens. Mr. Acheson kept to himself and so did his family until some of the boys joined us for football in Laidlaw's field and gradually, we got to know each other better. I got to know the eldest, Walter ('Wally') Acheson, when he served his time in Inchicore Works, although he was four or five years older than me. He was a motor bike enthusiast and I remember him showing me his best bike, which was a Triumph Twin 500 cc. One son, Harold Acheson, continued to farm there and also did work for the Guinnesses and for Conor Crowley. The farm was demolished in the 1980s and the Mulberry estate is built on that land.

The Carty family lived across the road from the Achesons' farm. A veteran of 1916, Tom Carty was among those deported after the surrender to England and released back home about a year later. Tom was a good painter and he used to help the priests in Porterstown Hall in setting up for plays and he often did the backdrops. When Tom was buried just inside the gate in Mulhuddart cemetery, shots were fired over his grave. He left behind three girls, Sheila, Eithne and Eileen. Sheila married and went to live abroad; Eithne and Eileen lived on in the house. Eithne married a Mr. Regan, who was involved in the prosthetics business and they raised their family in that house. The late artist, Charlie Whisker, and his former dress designer-cum-writer wife, Mariad, lived there afterwards, but it has long since been sold on.

Bradys' bungalow once stood in the field beside the Regans' house. Their land stretched across to a manor house, Laurel Lodge, known as 'Bradys' Farm.' A wooden stile near the entrance to Bradys' bungalow led to a path across the fields towards the Royal canal. In the 1930s, I used to walk this way with my father to Mass in Blanchardstown and he told me it was a right of way. The Laurel Lodge estate, built on these fields in the 1970s, takes its name from the house. The present College Gate estate was built in adjacent fields.

'Gregarnagh', former home of Crowley family and before that, the Fottrell family (the land has been cleared and the house is ready for demolition, 2017). Courtesy Reynolds Family Private Collection.

Another elegant manor house along the Carpenterstown Road was first owned by the Fottrell family who lived in the area since the 1930s. Mr. Fottrell had a solicitors' firm in town and owned the Tailtan Kennels. They were into dog breeding, in particular, Kerry Blues. In addition, they kept a herd of Jersey cows. Danny O'Gorman, who later married Kathleen Clarke, worked for Mr. Fottrell and drove their milk float, selling the milk locally. Many used a type of billy can called a 'sweetcan' to hold milk. Originally full of sweets, the 'sweetcan' was narrow with a handle but it held more milk than other receptacles. Mr. Fottrell owned a car when few had one, except during the war, when he rode a bicycle like everybody else. His bicycle had panniers. Their only child, Gwennie Fottrell, was a dog-lover and a sociable lady, always noted for her kindness in giving lifts to neighbours.

One day during the war, I was joined on my delivery round by my cousin, Frank Egan, who had come to visit. At a time when everybody had a weekly entitlement to 3½ ozs. of tea, Frank was carrying the Fottrells' tea ration, in a bag from a new consignment. When our handlebars accidentally locked together, the precious tea was at risk, but Frank managed to hold it high, avoiding a spillage. I was accustomed to keeping quiet inside Fottrells' gate, to avoid attracting the attention of dogs on the loose. However, as we approached Fottrells, Frank was regaling me with some story and I found it hard to curtail his high spirits. He finally took heed of my warning on being greeted by an angry pack of Kerry Blue dogs and we had to flee.

Mr. Fottrell sold his house to Conor Crowley, an accountant, and his wife Pat Crowley, a well-known fashion designer, who sometimes held private fashion shows there. The Crowleys rode out each morning and Conor Crowley also played polo in the Phoenix Park. When Pat Crowley sold up, she moved out towards Dolly's Lounge beyond Mulhuddart. Both Conor and Pat Crowley are now deceased and their former home is now set for re-development.

Having sold his house to the Crowleys, Mr. Fottrell built a long bungalow nearby, 'Garryknock,' with adjacent kennels. Alongside his bungalow, he built a dormer style house known as 'Sunday's Well,' where the O'Donoghue family lived. Bracken Park Drive is now built on the site of Sunday's Well. In order to maintain low density housing in the area, Mr. Fottrell bought up fields on both sides of the Carpenterstown Road. He sold off sites for detached houses and had detached houses built on the remaining land, which he sold on. The Bests, a sausage manufacturing family, lived in a detached house called 'Cottonwood,' now demolished and replaced by a small estate, appropriately called 'Cottonwood.' Adjacent to

Cottonwood is another small housing development called 'Woodberry.'

Further along the Carpenterstown Road, a mud lane led to a farmhouse with outbuildings where a man called Mooney lived with his sister in my time. I used to deliver a newspaper to them and had to negotiate up their laneway which had two deep ruts and a line of grass up the middle. When they died, Mr. Fottrell bought the property and an employee of his lived there. In the 1980s, detached houses were built along this lane which became known as 'Outfarm Lane.' The Butler family were among those who lived there together with Mrs. Butler's parents, the Kavanaghs, another sausage-manufacturing family.

Mr. Fottrell was a nice man who always had something interesting to tell when he gave you a lift. I remember him telling me that if a business had a clock, they risked prosecution if the clock didn't show the correct time. His strategy in buying up adjacent land was far-sighted as it succeeded in staving off development for his lifetime.

Mr. Mooney's brother lived in long bungalow on land fronting the Carpenterstown Road. He cycled to work in Dublin each day. When his wife died young, he was left with a large family. The eldest girl, Lil Mooney, mothered the children until she married herself. One of the girls, Patty Mooney, married a man called Mr. Madden and they lived on there with their three children. Six detached houses are now built on the site of Maddens' house. At the time of Ben Dunne's kidnapping in 1981, journalists descended upon the Mooney home to use their telephone, as mobile phones had not been invented at that stage.

Home of the Inglis family. In the background on the right are the houses that replaced the home of the Madden (Mooney) family. Courtesy Reynolds Family Private Collection.

A Mr. Clarke and his wife lived in a cottage adjacent to the Mooneys, which was owned by the Laidlaw family. When the Clarkes moved on, the Inglis family came to live there.

Other developments now built along the Carpenterstown road include 'Burnell' and 'Bramley.'

On the opposite side of the Carpenterstown Road, Mr. Fottrell acquired land from the Balfe family and built several detached houses. The Besson hotelier family lived in the first house before it was sold to the O'Ceallaigh family, who had a firm of solicitors. Dr. Solomon lived in the second detached house before selling it on to the Chatterton family, who had an extensive apple orchard behind the house. For years, a roadside sign flapped in the wind, *'Apples for Sale.'*

In the 1970s, Frank Dunne and Ben Dunne Junior, sons of Ben Dunne Senior of the renowned Dunnes Stores, came to live in Georgian-style houses built side-by-side, called 'The White House' and 'Winterwood' respectively. At that stage, the fields behind these houses stretched right across to Miss Betty Laidlaw's estate at Diswellstown and up to Porterstown.

At the site of Carpenter pub, a huge field extended from Coolmine to Porterstown, which I mentioned before. 'Guinness's airfield,' as we knew it, was owned by the Laidlaw family. Generally used for grazing cattle, it was also used by the Guinness family as a private airfield. Before the war, two hangars situated near the site of the Carpenter pub stored aircraft. Raphie Byrne's father minded the airfield - he lived in the first cottage on the lane to the left after the Coolmine railway gate. Raphie Byrne married Dolly Mooney and having emigrated to England, they eventually returning to live in Dunboyne.

Us kids knew that once a posh car or a taxi went up the Coolmine road, a plane was about to land or take off. It was usually the pilot coming to warm up the plane. If we missed the car, we'd still hear the sound of the engines starting up, which was enough to send us tearing up to watch. There was no runway - the planes took off from the grass. I remember myself and another fellow managed to get into a twelve-seater plane with six seats on either side. Of course, we took turns in the cockpit seats. Another time, I remember seeing an autogyro there. It required a short run for the autogyro to take off, but it could land straight down, like a helicopter.

Dolly Mooney told me that the kids in her family used to dash up to the airfield if they heard a plane engine. They knew there was a few shillings tip going if they were in time to open the double gate. By the end of the Second World War, the hangars had become dilapidated and eventually, they were removed. That land is now used as playing fields.

The Laidlaw family were of Scottish extraction from iron and cotton thread industrial backgrounds. They moved to the area at the beginning of the twentieth century and purchased three properties in the locality - Abbey Lodge, where the Manley family once lived, Diswellstown House, where Miss Betty Laidlaw lived, and Somerton, which they purchased from the Brooke family. Tom Laidlaw and his family lived at Somerton until the 1980s.

The entrance to Abbey Lodge was on a sharp right-angled bend in the road opposite where the Carpenter pub is situated. Douglas (Dougie) Laidlaw, a brother of Mr. T.K. Laidlaw of Somerton, lived at Abbey Lodge until the late 1920's, when he moved to the Riviera for his health. Between them, they trained horses, including *Gregalach* and *Grakle*, who went on to win the Aintree Grand National at Liverpool in 1929 and 1931 respectively, although they were no longer training them at that stage. The gate lodge was occupied by several families over the years, including the Morrisons - Mr. Morrison used to look after Dougie Laidlaw's horses. Eileen Morrison was in my class at school and at the age of 12, she contributed to the Schools Folklore Collection. Maureen Morrison was best friends with my older sister, Maureen.

While Mr. Laidlaw lived abroad, Abbey Lodge lay idle for years. Duncan Ferguson and his wife were caretakers who lived in the basement. Mr. Ferguson came up the steps for his newspaper; he spoke with a heavy Scottish accent. I used to cycle in through the main entrance and up the avenue lined with beech hedges and deliver their paper. Then I'd head across the extensive stable yard behind the house and out the back entrance near Coolmine railway. The yard had a grass square and a saddle room full of equestrian equipment, but it was empty of life. In a huge shed with sides half way down from the roof there were eight or nine boats rusting away - motor boats, sailing boats and more. I used to wish I had the use of one of them. Unlike the Guinness families of Knockmaroon and Farmleigh who always employed vigilant stewards, the Laidlaws were never bothered by locals crossing their property. Mr. Laidlaw returned to Ireland at the beginning of the war but to my recollection, he died before the war ended. The house was knocked down and housing estates called Bramley and Cherry Lawn were built on that land.

Taking you back to the Carpenter pub and on towards Coolmine, a small cottage on Malone's land was occupied by a Mr. and Mrs. Flynn. Paddy Malone later built a house on that site which then became a creche. Next was Malone's farm. Around 1928, Mr. Malone bought the farm which was in the townland of Sheepmore, Coolmine. Although he was an enterprising and successful farmer, he was known as a difficult man. He grew entire fields of brussel sprouts, turnips and other staple vegetables; his seven children, Terry, Jim, Paddy, Joe, John and two girls, helped on the farm from a young age. When World War II started, the Government brought in compulsory tillage, obliging those with farms and estates to grow food because of the dearth of imported goods, like grain from America. Mr. Malone bought a tractor when few owned tractors and had the tractor working day and night throughout the war.

Joe Malone told me that he used to plough fields on his own near Mulhuddart graveyard at night. As he furrowed towards the graveyard, the moon shone on the headstones, but once he turned the tractor around, he felt like looking over his shoulder when his back was to the graveyard. After the war, Mr. Malone was able to buy a brand-new car, a luxury in those days. Mr. Malone used to go to the barber for a hot shave with a cut-throat razor on Saturdays. Up to the 1970s, John and Joe Malone did a coal run in the area, operating from the outhouses on the farm. I remember asking them would they ever think of going back to farming, 'No way, slave labour,' they said. When the farm was sold off, the old farmhouse and outhouses were converted into a shop and a fuel merchant's and they became surrounded by the Warren, Luttrell Park and Riverwood estates. Eventually, the old farm buildings were also demolished for housing. Many Malone descendants live on in the area.

Opposite the entrance to Malone's farm, Jack Thompson, a market gardener, lived in a cottage with his sister. His land was well-tilled and his frontage stretched a good distance along the road.

Mrs. Phillippa built a detached dormer bungalow on Abbey Lodge land, with its gable end to the Coolmine Road. She used to pass by in a green chauffeur-driven Rover car with her big white poodles sitting upright beside her on the back seat. Mrs. Phillippa's chauffeur lived in the gate lodge where the Morrison family had once lived.

The farmyard entrance to Abbey Lodge was near the Coolmine railway gate. Directly across the road from that farmyard entrance was Abbey Cottage, owned by the Eager family. The Eager family have an association with Coolmine going back to the 1800s. Mr. Eager worked in the Ordnance Survey in the Phoenix Park and he reared cattle on his farm, which extended back considerably towards the canal bank. He had two sons, one was Robert Eager, who worked in Hills Mills in Lucan. His wife, Charlotte, worked for the Guinness family. Later on, Jim Bolger, the trainer, lived there and stabled his horses in outbuildings at the back of the house. In the very early hours, we used to hear the horses trotting by, heading for the gallops in the Phoenix Park.

Two adjoining cottages abutted the railway. Mr. Byrne who operated the railway gate occupied the first cottage. Late at night, passersby sometimes operated the gate themselves, first manoeuvring the signal about 200 yards away which was hard enough to do, and next, opening and closing both gates. Paddy Brennan and his large family including Marie, Rose, Stephen and Paddy lived in the second cottage. Paddy Brennan worked for Jimmy Mangan on the Clonsilla Road. Rose Brennan married Leo Clarke, brother of Kathleen O'Gorman.

In the 1970s after Mrs. Byrne became widowed, a long term dispute meant that the Coolmine railway gate was shut each night and motorists had to find an alternative route.

Beyond Coolmine railway gate, Kirkpatrick Bridge has a plaque on it dated 1795. Alex Kirkpatrick, from Scottish wool merchant stock and a director of the Royal Canal, owned land in Coolmine until the 1920s. The Kirkpatrick family lived in Coolmine House which was demolished in the 1970s. Scoil Oilibhear now stands on the Coolmine Demesne.

Towpath along the Royal Canal. Courtesy Reynolds Family Private Collection.

Kennan Bridge. Courtesy Reynolds Family Private Collection.

At one time, the laneway beside the bridge continued on as a track negotiable by foot along the canal, all the way to the old Dickensian-style schoolhouse in Clonsilla. Several families lived along this laneway. Barney Hall and his wife lived in a cottage with a galvanised tin roof on the corner of the laneway. It is now gone, replaced by a newly built two-storey house. Next was the home of the Balfe family. Mrs. Balfe reared turkeys and my mother always bought her Christmas turkey from Mrs. Balfe. For years, Willie Balfe worked in Lord Moyne's and he used to be up and down the Coolmine Road on his tractor. Across from the Balfes was Gilbert Howe, a relation of theirs. I do not recall the names of others who lived along the lane. Along the Royal Canal near Porterstown, a favourite deep pool for swimming was located at a place we knew as 'McGovern's Rocks' – it was rocky rather than muddy underfoot at that point.

Let's head back down to the Coolmine Road. A pair of cottages once stood directly opposite the laneway but I have no recollection who lived in them. Rose Cottage was further on towards Coolmine Cross. It was a rose-covered house with a chocolate-box appearance and a balustrade-style front wall. My father was interested in buying that house at one stage, but nothing came of it. A walled avenue led up to Woodview House, a maudlin-looking place, owned by a Miss Sadie Ellis, who let out rooms to lodgers. Then there was Rockfield House in Coolmine. The 1923 Thom's Directory records a W. Hoare as the owner of Rockfield. The house is now demolished but Rockfield has been used to name newer roads in the area.

McDonalds's farm was on the opposite side of the road, closer to Coolmine Cross. Their large farm house was set among trees and its entrance was on the Clonsilla Road, pretty near to the crossroads. Glenville, Brompton and Delwood are located on what was once McDonald's farm. Two of the McDonald ladies went to live in a bungalow in the laneway between Godley's drapery and T.P. O'Reilly's butcher shop, off Main Street, Blanchardstown.

Coolmine Cross was once a full crossroads with through roads. The road directly across from the Coolmine Road was the heavily wooded Grove Road. Over thirty years ago, the Council erected a wall which blocked off traffic to Grove Road. In my time, there were three houses along Grove Road, including a grand house owned by the Jellett family, who had an estate there. Mainie Jellett is a well-known Irish artist. Coolmine Community School is there now as well as Coolmine House, a drug treatment centre.

Cycling in the direction of Clonsilla, Jelletts back lodge was behind farm gates on the right. I am not sure who lived there. Jimmy Mangan lived next on the right.

Jimmy Mangan and Shem Cullen's house on the Clonsilla Road (now demolished).

There was a petrol pump outside his house. Shem Cullen came to live in Jimmy Mangan's house. Shem used to keep a blazing fire going and he took a saw to his armchair and shortened the legs so he could get the full blast of heat from the fire. Shem used to meet up with Parky Ludlow and Lar Kane for lunch. After Shem died around 2010, the house was demolished.

The Proudfoot family lived in a cottage on a corner located near the ESB sub-station. I never remember the parents but when a sister of my father's, Josie Reynolds, married Peter Proudfoot, I came to know the family well. There was Molly Proudfoot and several brothers - Mick, John, Tony, Joe, Frank and Peter. Peter and Josie made their home in Clonsilla. Their daughter, Kathleen Proudfoot, married Chick Curry and they went to live in Palmerstown. Chick and my cousin Peter Reynolds used to get together for musical arrangements. I am not sure if Proudfoots' cottage was on Vincentian land but the national school in Clonsilla was built on Vincentian land.

Former home of the Proudfoot family, Clonsilla Road. Courtesy Reynolds Family Private Collection.

Right opposite the junction of the road leading to Porterstown, I delivered a newspaper to two elderly Protestant ladies, the Miss Mackeys, who lived in an ivy-covered house. One in particular always answered the door and I remember her well as she never failed to give a tip at Christmas. Their farm was worked by farm labourers.

Castleknock – Memories of a Neighbourhood

Myself and Austin Fagan often cycled up to the library. I remember one day in particular during the war seeing a German plane high in the sky on the way home. The Irish were firing at the plane and you could see bursts of explosives – although Ireland was neutral, we used to fire at the planes in a bid to re-direct them back towards the Irish sea. Back at home, the family had heard a noise on the roof and when I got up there, I found a piece of shrapnel that had fallen from the sky.

A long corner building, two bungalows, stood across from The Thatch, one which housed the Post Office. The telephone number for Clonsilla Post Office back then was *Clonsilla 1*. A chap called O'Neill lived in that long building and I knew him from school in Castleknock. He was very tall and a good footballer but unusually, he was not a member of the CYMS.

There were several handsome residences in Clonsilla, including Clonsilla House, where Portersgate is now situated, once owned by Captain Steed and later, by Judge Wylie. Other grand houses in the area included Clonsilla Lodge, Beech Park and Clinfield, later called Lohunda House. Built in 1909, Lohunda House was occupied by a Mr. Hilliard, who had stables. The entrance to Lohunda Demesne is opposite the Spar shop (originally The Thatch) in Clonsilla. In the shade of mature beech trees, the gate lodge is all that remains today. Later on, Sir Hugh Nugent trained winners at Lohunda and after him, Jim Bolger was successful in training championship race horses for both national hunt and flat racing. The Porterstown and Clonsilla soil was rich with limestone, copper iron and manganese, which made it an excellent area for horse breeding. Horse training was an important source of employment in the area and many of the trainers were known to us.

Photograph of long building which housed former Post Office. Courtesy Reynolds Private Family Collection.

Tony Reynolds

Gate Lodge to Lohunda. Courtesy Reynolds Family Private Collection.

The Cunningham family had a sawmill and some land at Kellystown in Clonsilla. A successful undertaking business developed out of that and they were the sole undertakers serving the wide area of Clonsilla, Castleknock, Blanchardstown, Mulhuddart, Ashtown, Chapelizod and beyond. There were about six Cunningham lads - six footers - all older than me, who gave their father a hand to run the business, so there was never a shortage of a pall bearer. The youngest, Bobby Cunningham, was the local heart throb. 'Whistler' Cunningham, whose real name was Jim, was a bit of a character. Cunninghams' funeral business is still on the go today, although it has been much expanded.

```
Cunningham Mrs. B., 7 Clifton tce., Monkstown...  8 2728
Cunningham Bros. Coffin Mfrs. Undertkrs..Clonsilla     8
CUNNINGHAM BROS. Ltd. Wire Metal Workers,
   125 Francis st.............................................. 5 1137
Cunningham Mrs. Catherine, Cafe, 3 Burgh qy.... 7 2023
Cunningham & Co. Ltd. Wholesale Warehousemen
   46 Sth. William st......................................... 7 0163
Cunningham Des., 25 Oaklands cres., Rathgar...... 9 5433
Cunningham Mrs. E., 3 Carlton villas, Shelbourne rd 6 3463
Cunningham Edward, Grocery Provision Merchant,
   Ballygall rd. W........................................... 34 1023
Cunningham Miss E. H., Treo, Churchtown rd...... 90 8126
Cunningham F. J., Pawnbroker & Jeweller,
   6 Upr. Erne st............................................. 6 5569
Cunningham Mrs. G. M., 7 Dunluce rd., Clontarf... 33 4093
Cunningham Mrs. H. A., 56 Nth. Brunswick st....  7 9517
```

Left: Row of houses, Larch Grove Clonsilla. Courtesy Reynolds Family Private Collection. Right: Cunningham's telephone number was Clonsilla 8. Accessed from the 1954 Telephone Directory, Little Museum of Dublin.

The Lynch family lived in the tudor style house situated in an island near the Protestant Church at the centre of Clonsilla.

Left: Lynch family home, Clonsilla. Right: St. Mary's Protestant Church, Clonsilla. Courtesy Reynolds Family Private Collection.

St. Mary's Protestant Church in the centre of Clonsilla was built in 1845, with the tower being added five years later. The church houses an Evie Hone stained glass window depicting St. Fiacra, the patron saint of gardeners. Although the church is only yards from the main road, it is a very peaceful place. Apparently the land on which the church stands has an ecclesiastical history going back to 500 A.D. The graveyard is near to capacity; anyone wanting to be buried there has to have a connection with the area.

The Thom's Directory of 1957 showed the following residents in Church View, Clonsilla, adjacent to St. Mary's Church (12 County Council Cottages):-

Byrne, B.	Smith, P.
Hughes, R.	Proudfoot, P.
Dempsey, W.	O'Brien, J.
Buggle, J.	Dignam, M.
Telford, Joseph	Thornberry, B
McDonnell,	Bonass, R.

St. Joseph's Hospital in Clonsilla was established in 1943, following the acquisition of a small country mansion, The Grange, by the Daughters of Charity. It provides a range of services for people with intellectual disabilities.

Clonsilla Signal Station and Railway gate beside bridge. Courtesy Reynolds Family Private Collection.

Up and over the hill at Clonsilla railway station. Iarnrod Éireann have preserved the signal and control box. The signal box is composed of a glazed timber-clad office raised over a red brick base. The level crossing gates and the signals of yesteryear were manually operated 24/7.

After the tracks is a house with a corrugated tin roof. To my recollection, Tommy Bennett lived there. Tommy was a gunman for sport and right-hand man to Maxwell Arnott, the horse trainer. My mother knew Tommy as he had worked at Belleville stables, near where her people lived in Ashtown. Tommy drove a car and used to wear a smart sports coat and a racing-style cap. Maxwell Arnott was related to the Arnott family of department store fame and he came to Clonsilla in the 1920s to train horses after a brief commission in the British Army. He acquired a house known as The Cottage opposite St. Joseph's Hospital in Clonsilla. Maxwell was a philantrophic man who always contributed to local causes. Next door was Greenmount, occupied by Captain Martin who had two sons, one who was a keen polo player. Maxwell Arnott later came into possession of Greenmount House. He gave good employment in the area, to vets and suppliers of oats, hay and other requirements for horses, as well as to jockeys – I remember two in particular, Mickey Gordon and Nick O'Leary.

Greenmount House, Clonsilla. Courtesy Reynolds Family Private Collection.

Depending on what customers were on the paper round, sometimes there was no need to go right into Clonsilla village, so instead, I took the road to Porterstown past Clonsilla's forge which is still there today, aptly called 'Old Forge.' Christy Hughes lived here along with his brother and his sister Gretta. Gretta played badminton in the CYMS and she also made a contribution to The Schools Collection in the 1930s. Christy was sixty years in the undertaking business and lived to a great age.

The Old Forge in Clonsilla. Courtesy Reynolds Family Private Collection.

The Old School in Clonsilla. Courtesy Reynolds Family Private Collection.

A short distance on is the Dickensian-style school in Clonsilla, with living quarters, which opened in 1853 and closed its doors in 1963.

The school looms tall on the bank of the Royal Canal at a point where a tragedy occurred in 1845 when sixteen lives were lost when the passage boat 'Longford' sank. It was said the steersman went below to dine and committed the rudder to the charge of a boy on board the boat. A plaque on the bridge records the tragedy.

The entrance to Lar Kane's is directly across from Clonsilla School and Lar's brother lived in a house behind with his family. At one time, a pathway past Kanes led all the way to Kirkpatrick Bridge at Coolmine. The railway cottage is now abandoned but the path on the opposite bank of the canal is still well-used. The fields beyond the railway are home to St. Mochta's Soccer Club.

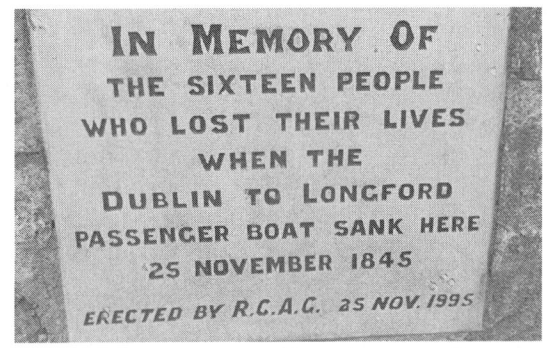

In the 1930s, Josie Kane made a contribution to The Schools Folklore Collection.

Plaque on bridge. Courtesy Reynolds Family Private Collection.

Home of Lar Kane. Courtesy Reynolds Family Private Collection.

Abandoned Railway Cottage. Courtesy Reynolds Family Private Collection.

Next we go down the road towards Porterstown to deliver a paper to a farmer, Mr. Lynam, whose farm is now derelict. I knew 'Lecky' Lynam, who was a good athlete, although he was a bit older than me.

Lynam farm now derelict. Courtesy Reynolds Family Private Collection.

Further on, the Mooney family lived in Holm Ville which is still there. Mr. Mooney was a talented builder who built our shop. His daughter, Hilda Mooney, was a friend of my older sister, Maureen. Hilda and her sister Ita both made contributions to The Schools Folklore Collection in the 1930s.

Holmville, home of the Mooney family. Courtesy Reynolds Family Private Collection.

A Parish site in between these two properties contains the remains of the old Porterstown church. The new St. Mochta's church at Porterstown had been built around 1870 and later on, a parish house was built beside it. It was always a bone of contention among parishioners that no community hall or playing fields had been provided in the parish. Neither Connolly's Hall in Blanchardstown nor Horan's hall in Clonsilla were parish properties and the playing fields behind The Greyhound Bar in Blanchardstown were owned by the Carroll family. When Father Cogan chose to build a parish hall on the site of the old church between Porterstown and Clonsilla, people kicked up on the grounds it was too far away, but building went ahead anyway. This big hall was always called 'the new hall.' It was mainly used for dances and plays. Some drama groups came out from town and put on plays. About ten years after it was erected, the 'new hall' burnt down and after that, the small hall was refurbished for use. Of course, CYMS membership was exclusive to men and it is notable that many CYMS members were older men. It was only open to women for badminton and dances. When the *'new'* hall burnt down, the small hall was refurbished. It continued to be used by the CYMS and the scoutmaster, Jack Lovely, got permission for the scouts to meet there.

11.
OUTINGS

Going on holiday was unheard of when I was growing up. Nobody of our acquaintance went on holidays except those with country roots who took a break back at the old homestead. Country cousins often visited in turn. Our family knew nobody that lived down the country and in any event, we were very much restricted by the shop which opened every day. Day trips and outings were our big treats.

On hot days, my mother took us to the beach, usually to Bray but sometimes to Killiney Beach or Howth. Our Aunt Jen used to board the Luttrellstown bus at Ashtown and we'd make our way on into Tara Street Station to get the train or to Eden Quay to catch the bus to Howth. Sometimes we'd meet up with our Aunt Fanny and our Egan cousins, all pre-arranged by letter. We'd converge on the beach at Bray or Killiney.

Bray was considered a relatively upmarket seaside resort. Many of the Victorian seafront houses took in paying guests and bands used to play at the bandstand on the promenade. We jostled in the queues for ice cream cones or candy floss or sticks of pink rock with the name 'Bray' circled on the inner white barrel. Whenever we went to Bray, we had our tea in a tea shop at the end of the promenade, near the incline to Bray Head. We'd have fun in the amusement arcade, at the shooting gallery, taking the ghost tour, or at the carnival. We'd ride on chair-o-planes, dodgems, swinging boats or on the fairy wheel - 'hurdy-gurdies,' we called them. On trips to Killiney, we brought a picnic - flasks and sandwiches - as there were no food venues there. Portmarnock was not well known and it was sparsely populated. The one time we went to Portmarnock, we were washed out of it and had to shelter in half-built houses.

Left: Tony Reynolds on a day trip to Bray c. 1940. Right: Donkey ride at Bray. My sisters, Geraldine & Carmel, c. 1944. Courtesy Reynolds Family Private Collection.

Most years, we went to the Zoo, in through the thatched kiosk entrance where we bought nuts for the monkeys in a long cone made of newspaper. We usually had the nuts eaten by the time we reached the monkey house. You could feed the elephants too - experience the rough trunk landing on the palm of your hand. You could ride on the back of an elephant or on a cart pulled by two miniature ponies. Feeding time was always a spectacle - the keeper arriving with buckets of fish for the sealions, the chimps tea party on the lawn and the penguins performing all sorts of stunts to grab food, sliding on their bellies across wet rocks. The keeper at the snake house took out snakes and placed them around your neck so you could have your photo taken. On one visit, my mother turned around and caught my brother, Noel, with his finger in through the grid of a cage, petting the nose of a wolf.

A few years ago, I had to collect something from the Zoo. I went gingerly through the goods entrance opposite the Garda Headquarters and spotted a lady tending a garden. I decided to ask her the way. It turned to be the older sister of Mona Clarke – a girl who had been in school with me – she had married the foreman over the Zoo grounds. Her brother, Tommy Clarke, also worked in the Zoo. When I came across John Nolan from Clonsilla who used to play snooker with me in the CYMS, I said to him, *"Is this where you've been hiding all these years?"*

The Phoenix Park was always a great venue for family outings and sporting fixtures and for those who preferred music, bands played regularly at the bandstand in The Hollow, near to the Zoo entrance. A large open plain known as the Fifteen Acres accommodates football matches. There's a polo ground at the boundary of the Zoo and a cricket ground nearby. The Park was always shut off for special events like cycling and running races and for motor racing, when the day started off with motorcycle racing and went on to motor car racing. The racing cars were built like tanks with extended bonnets and they were driven by world-class drivers. The cars used a clockwise course, zooming down Chesterfield Avenue towards Castleknock, but they had to slow down before Mountjoy corner in order to negotiate the turn for Ashtown gate. Needless to say, every young lad in the area pretended to be a motor racing driver in the days following the event. The racing stopped during World War II but it was revived again in 1949.

The air display was the biggest annual event in the years leading up to the war. There was a small admission charge at the Park gates. The pilots were ex-servicemen from World War I and it was mostly bi-planes in the pageant. Not alone was there the spectacle of loop-the-loop stunts and parachute jumps, but for 2s 6d, (mere cents these days), you could take a plane ride with two or three people. The pilot usually circled the Phoenix Park before touching down again.

Two exceptional events drew massive crowds to the Phoenix Park. One such event was the Eucharistic Congress held in 1932. Every house, shop and church was festooned with bunting, flower baskets and flags and many an altar was built. Although I was only five, I remember my father putting up a flagpole and hoisting a yellow and white papal flag where a big beech tree stood at the hut beside our house. I have a recollection of being at the Eucharistic Congress with my mother, who was pushing a pram, and the presence of a huge amount of motor cars. The other big event was the visit of Pope John Paul II in 1979. A papal cross stands on the spot in the Fifteen Acres where he celebrated Mass and talked to the people of Ireland.

The local sports day in Blanchardstown was another annual outing on our calendar. The Carroll family owned the pub along Blanchardstown's Main Street, now called the Greyhound Bar. They also owned the athletic field behind the pub, known in my time as 'Carroll's Field'. All sorts of sporting events were held there including running and the long jump and they also had pitches for football and hurling. There's a supermarket on that land now.

Tony Reynolds in scout's uniform, O'Connell Bridge, Dublin. Courtesy Reynolds Family Private Collection.

Having joined the scouts at the age of 11½ in 1939, the annual camping trip quickly came on the horizon. However, myself and T.P. O'Reilly, who were the same age, were turned down, deemed too young for the trip. When the scoutmaster, Jim Lovely, eventually relented, a group of about eighteen of us scouts went on the train to Arklow. In addition to Jim, who was in charge, my cousins, Peter and Tommy Reynolds, were on the trip, as well as 'Parky' Kelly who was a good deal older than me, and Kevin Kelly, who was about seventeen, and Mickey Harford. We camped for two weeks near the beach, north of the Avoca river. Despite wartime rationing, we managed to feed ourselves for two weeks. Every day, two scouts were put on catering duty, usually a younger lad with an older lad, my companion being Kevin Kelly from Peck's Lane. We had to peel the spuds and vegetables for the entire brigade and then we made a fire with sticks or we used our primus stove to heat the pots of grub.

As children, we took long spins on our bikes as far as Dunboyne or Clonee or Maynooth and had an ice cream before heading home. As adults, we cycled further afield. Punctures were a regular feature of life. Generally, cyclists mended their own punctures but if a tyre needed repair, it had to be brought over to Glass's garage in Blanchardstown.

L to R: Tony Reynolds, Noel Christian, Tom Christian (boy scout on right), and Noel Reynolds (front). Courtesy Reynolds Family Private Collection.

My brother Noel Reynolds on his bicycle. Courtesy Reynolds Family Private Collection.

Larry Reynolds (cousin), Noel Reynolds (brother) and Joe Curry on a day trip. Courtesy Reynolds Family Private Collection.

Castleknock – Memories of a Neighbourhood

One summer, myself and my cousin, Peter Reynolds, cycled to Laytown on a camping holiday. As the scouts were set to arrive on the last weekend, and overlap with our stay, they put their tents on the train for us to collect at Laytown train station and let us use them in the meantime. Another cousin, Padraig (Pat) Egan, who had no experience of cycling, came after work on a bike. I remember him collapsing on to a grassy bank to recover after the journey. Although they were both cousins of mine, they didn't know each other as they were from opposite sides of the family.

We camped for two weeks in a field at the Grotto Wood, with the kind permission of Mr. Delaney, a racehorse trainer. Our tent was pitched alongside the river, on a grassy promontory on the Dublin side of Laytown beach. We swam in the sea or the river in lieu of a wash. Each day, the three of us used to split up to see what food we could forage from the local shops. The shopkeepers were appalled at our chosen campsite because the Grotto Wood was supposed to be haunted. Now Padraig could be meticulous; he had taken the trouble to mention at the start of the holiday that he was particular about hygiene. Then we discovered an earwig in our milk bottle one morning. I certainly wasn't walking all the way into Laytown for a fresh bottle, so I picked the earwig out of the bottle and used the milk. Peter followed suit. So did Padraig.

With charming manners and good looks, Padraig was a great man for getting off his mark with the ladies. He was the only chap I ever knew that got to leave home three girls in one night. We frequented a ramshackle dancehall between Bettystown and Mornington called 'The Burrows.' Having taken to the floor with a lady, Padraig came over to me after a short time. *"Back soon, this girl has to be home early."* Off he went. About a half an hour later, I was up dancing myself when I spotted Padraig dancing with another lady. He came over to me again. *"Back soon, I'm leaving this girl home."* Off he went again. He arrived back in the hall as things were wrapping up. Outside, our bikes were heaped together in a big mound, with handlebars entangled. Padraig went to the assistance of a lady, extricated her bike from the mound and stood chatting to her. He left that girl home too.

Another night, Padraig and I cycled to a marquee dance ten miles away in Duleek. Peter decided to stay put. Padraig met a young lady called Florina at the dance, who asked could she cycle home with us, which was no problem, as she was travelling in our direction. When we reached her place, I hung back discreetly while Padraig saw her home. We had both gathered she lived in the gate lodge but to our surprise, she lived in the big house. When we arrived back to our ghostly campsite, Peter was sorry he hadn't come along. Shortly after our holiday, Florina whisked Padraig off to the Military Tattoo – the tickets were like gold dust. There the romance ended.

Another time, I went with my cousin and regular companion, Tommy Reynolds, on a holiday to Blackpool, a mecca for girls. After the ferry and train trips, we arrived with no accommodation booked. We tried a street full of guesthouses, one of us on either side of the road. We'd shake our heads across to one another when we had no luck – it seemed all the accommodation was booked. Eventually, we did get digs and we had a fantastic holiday, making full use of the renowned Tower ballroom, Empress Ballroom and the Winter Gardens. We had brought along a few pounds of butter which was appreciated by our landlady as butter was scarce.

Given the number of racehorse trainers living in the vicinity and the proximity to the Phoenix Park racecourse, it was not surprising that going to the races became popular as we got older. As well as catching the evening meetings at the Phoenix Park racecourse, it was not too far to Fairyhouse, The Curragh, Leopardstown and Punchestown. It made the outing more attractive if you had a hot tip for a race. I bought a great pair of field glasses in a pawnbroker's shop at the bottom of Harcourt Street which had three sets of lens, including one for the field and another for astronomy. One day, I opened the Irish Independent to see a picture of myself at The Curragh with the field glasses up against my face.

My brother, Noel Reynolds, camping with friends (there were no chalet-style or igloo-style tents back then). Courtesy Reynolds Family Private Collection.

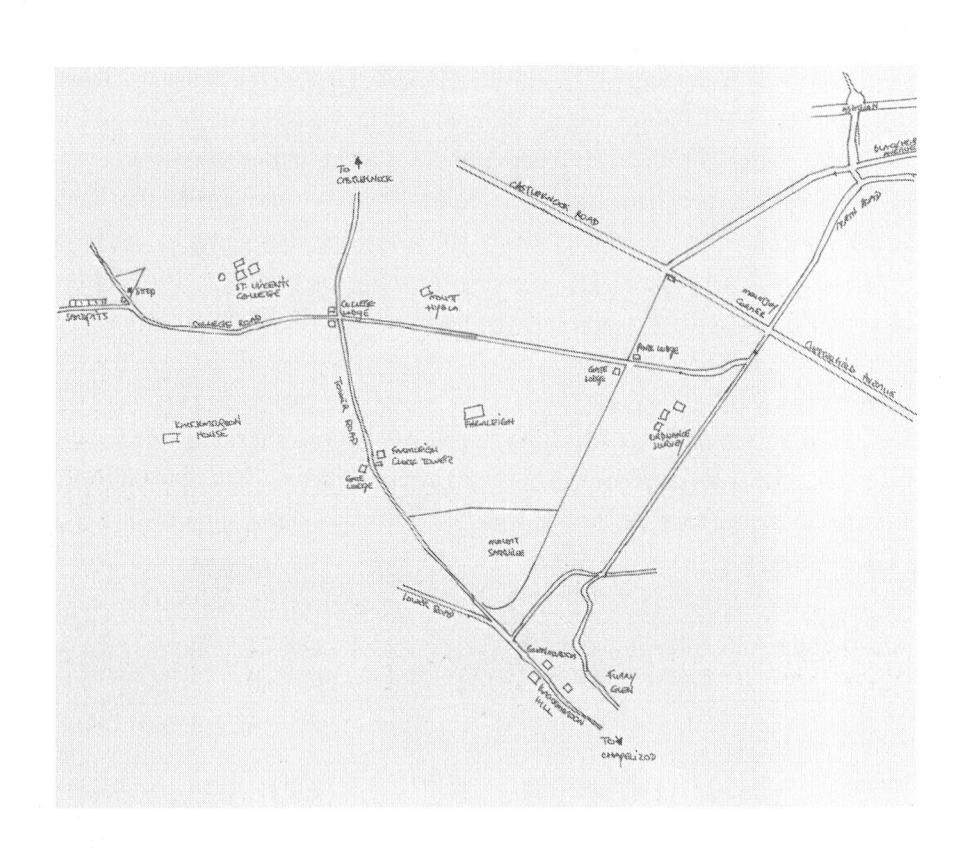

12.
THE FARMLEIGH NEWSPAPER RUN

The Farmleigh newspaper round took in residents on Lord Iveagh's estate and workers living in the Phoenix Park. My usual route by bicycle was along the College Road as far as the College Lodge, where I took a right turn past the front gate lodge of Lord Moyne's estate, Knockmaroon. Off I cycled down the Tower Road in the direction of Chapelizod, but I only went as far as the Clock Tower.

Knockmaroon Gate Lodge, Guinness Knockmaroon Estate, Tower Road (across the road from Farmleigh's Clock Tower, Tower Road, 2017). Courtesy Reynolds Family Private Collection.

161

Castleknock – Memories of a Neighbourhood

Farmleigh's Clock Tower, Tower Road. Courtesy Reynolds Family Private Collection.

Visible for miles, the Clock Tower stands at two hundred feet, high above Farmleigh's mature trees. Topped by a revolving weathercock vane, it is actually a water tower, providing a private water supply for the estate. The Lennon family lived in the gate lodge at Farmleigh's Clock Tower. The Kavanaghs lived at the Knockmaroon gate lodge across the road – their son, John Kavanagh, was a bit older than me. The Higgins family moved there later from Castleknock village.

In 1873, the present Lord Iveagh's great grandfather bought Farmleigh, an estate of 78 acres. Farmleigh's main entrance opens directly into the Phoenix Park beside White's Gate. Lord Iveagh's

Gate Lodge, Farmleigh's Clock Tower entrance, Tower Road, 2017. Courtesy Reynolds Family Private Collection.

principal estate is at Elveden in England, so he only lived in Farmleigh for part of the year. As well as heading up the Guinness brewery, the family had a philanthropic record and their legacy to Dublin is still intact today. They set up the 'Iveagh Trust' which contributed to slum clearance, urban renewal housing projects, the creation of public parks and many other projects. In 1927, Guinness named their first barge *Farmleigh* and their later fleet fondly commemorated local places names - *Knockmaroon, Chapelizod, Castleknock* and *Clonsilla*.

The Iveagh children were educated in England but sometimes, they travelled on the Luttrellstown bus. Lord Iveagh owned Farmleigh until it was controversially bought by the Government in the 1999 for €29.2 million. Refurbished at a cost of about €23 million, it is now managed by the Office of Public Works and hosts scheduled events and conferences as well as accommodating visiting dignitaries.

On up the avenue and straight up to the front portico door of Farmleigh, where a retainer answered the door or sometimes, he'd be out front waiting on the newspaper. After delivering at the big house, I cycled down the long avenue, past the ornamental lake and out through Farmleigh's main entrance gate. Farmleigh is well known for its walled garden and sunken garden.

Farmleigh, former Guinness home of Lord Iveagh, now owned by OPW, open to the public. Courtesy Reynolds Family Private Collection.

Lodge at Farmleigh's main entrance at White's Gate, Phoenix Park, 2017. Courtesy Reynolds Family Private Collection.

Park Lodge, White's Gate, Phoenix Park, former home of Fred Fisher, 2017. Courtesy Reynolds Family Private Collection.

In the Phoenix Park, I delivered a newspaper to the park keeper, Fred Fisher, who lived at Park Lodge, beside White's Gate. Back on the bike again, I pedalled across to the Ordnance Survey and went in through the gates to deliver papers to four or five residents there. When they upped security for some reason at the Ordnance Survey, deliveries had to be left with the gateman. It suited me fine as it made the round quicker.

Originally, the Ordnance Survey building was home to Lord Mountjoy. It was later converted into a cavalry barracks called Mountjoy Barracks. This is how the nearby crossroads junction at Chesterfield Avenue became known as Mountjoy corner. In 1824, the Ordnance Survey of Ireland (OSI) took up residence and officers had charge of a survey that mapped Ireland for valuation and taxation purposes. After 1998, military involvement with the Ordnance Survey was phased out. Over the years, the building expanded to include a print works and a shop with maps for sale that is still open to the public.

Out the Ordnance Survey gate and back into the Phoenix Park. The next delivery was to the park deerkeeper, who lived at Rose Cottage, a detached hexagonal-shaped cottage surrounded by a high hedge. The cottage is unchanged today.

The Park was lit with traditional gas lamps which required the gas lighter man

Gate Lodge at entrance to Ordnance Survey, Phoenix Park, 2017. Courtesy Reynolds Family Private Collection.

Rose Cottage, Phoenix Park, 2017. Courtesy Reynolds Family Private Collection.

Castleknock Gate, Phoenix Park. Courtesy Brendan Costello, showing his wife, 'Peggy' Costello.

to cycle from lamppost to lamppost each evening on his gas lighting round. The job of gas lighter was passed from father-to-son in certain families. The gatekeepers wore uniforms and they were obliged to abide by certain regulations while living in Park premises, for instance, they were prohibited from keeping animals. The Phoenix Park has its own piece of legislation, the Phoenix Park Act, 1925, with a set of bye-laws which includes a list of gate opening and closing times and other rules, for example, a ban on commercial vehicles entering the Park. The only Park gates left open after 11.00 p.m. were those at either end of Chesterfield Avenue – at Parkgate Street and Castleknock. Until the 1990s, White's Gate was open to vehicular traffic during daytime hours. Back in the day, it was a quick route through the Park and into town, with a driver encountering only three sets of traffic lights before O'Connell Street – at Queen Street, Church Street and Capel Street. The Office of Public Works closed the gate permanently as a means of traffic control.

The Park has been home to a free-roaming population of deer since the 1600s but until the 1970s, cattle were grazed there over the summer months, which kept the grass down. The cattle owners paid a tariff and the cattle were tagged and branded for identification and inspection purposes. As cattle straying onto the roads were causing a hazard to motorists and injuries to man and beast, the practice of grazing cattle in the park was discontinued.

Farmleigh's farmyard entrance, White's Road, 2017 (known locally as Weekes's Road). Courtesy Reynolds Family Private Collection.

Nearly done. It was a homeward run out White's Gate and down White's Road, which we always knew as 'Weekes's Road.' On past Farmleigh's farmyard, where many of Lord Iveagh's estate workers lived, including Mrs. Dempsey, the Hand family and the steward, Mr. Palmer.

The next house, Mount Hybla, in Georgian style, was the Glebe House for the Church of Ireland parish of Castleknock until 1938, when the rector moved into a house beside the dispensary in Castleknock village. After the rector left, the Manager of Lucan Dairies lived at Mount Hybla. A dairy herd used to graze in the surrounding fields. Lucan Dairies had its premises in Parkgate Street. Judge O'Connor, who had lived at Castlemount, took up residence in a new house on a site bordering Mount Hybla. Mount Hybla is now a nursing home.

Mount Hybla, White's Road 2017, now a nursing home. Courtesy Reynolds Family Private Collection.

Through the crossroads at the College Lodge and down the College Road brought me home.

However, if instead of turning in at Farmleigh's Clock Tower, I continued on towards Chapelizod, I'd pass several places of interest along the way.

Along Tower Road, Castlemount is a castellated house with towers and magnificent views over the Liffey valley. The German Koenig family, who owned the Wicklow Hotel, built Castlemount around 1830 and called it Schlossburg - it was later re-named Castlemount. It has a parapet over the door and cast iron boot

Castlemount, Tower Road. Courtesy of the National Inventory of Architectural Heritage.

Mount Sackville, Tower Road. Courtesy Reynolds Family Private Collection.

scrapers at the granite steps. The gate lodge is rendered with piers on both sides and cast iron gates. The Koenig family later moved to the Oatlands estate, along the road to Porterstown. Owned at one stage by the Guinness family, Judge O'Connor lived there until he moved to White's Road and then Judge Buchanan lived there.

Beyond Castlemount, steps lead down to a house overlooking the Liffey Valley where Mr. and Mrs. Higginbotham lived. Mr. Higginbotham always lifted his hat to say, 'good day.' The couple used to drive over to deal in our shop.

Mount Sackville is a forty-acre property bordering the Phoenix Park at the Knockmaroon gate. It is a fee-paying school for girls which at one time accommodated boarders. Formerly owned by Lord George Sackville, from whom Sackville Street got its name, it has been run by a French order of Catholic nuns, the Sisters of St. Joseph of Cluny, since 1864.

Glenmaroon Gate Lodge, beside the Knockmaroon gate of the Phoenix Park. Courtesy REA Coonan (Maynooth) WK Nowlan Property.

The neo-gothic cut stone lodge to Glenmaroon stands beside the Knockmaroon gate of the Phoenix Park. A chap called Gerry Willoughby once lived in this lodge.

Glenmaroon, home of the Guinness family. Courtesy REA Coonan (Maynooth) WK Nowlan Property.

In the early 1900s, the Honourable Arthur Ernest Guinness, of brewery fame, bought a house that sits on grounds of just under five and a half acres, Knockmaroon House. Arthur married an aristocratic society lady, Marie Clothilde Russell, and work got under way to make their home luxurious. The fairytale Tudor Revival design had a 'smoking lounge' and an indoor swimming pool. Arthur's heiress daughters, Aileen, Maureen and Oonagh, were known as the 'Golden Guinness Girls.' With eight husbands between them, their antics inspired the gossip pages. Aileen Guinness went on to live in Luttrellstown Castle.

The main house has a portico-style entrance opening into a baronial panelled hallway and decorative red earth chimney pots in barley twist style. The property comprises two buildings, one each side of Knockmaroon Hill. The buildings were collectively re-named Glenmaroon, or Glenmaroon House. Guinness staff occupied the building on the south side while the family lived at Glenmaroon House, on the north side, abutting the Phoenix Park. After Arthur Guinness died in 1949, the property passed to the Irish State to pay death duties and it became the subject of a court case in 1951 related to those duties. In the 1950s, the

Sisters of Charity renovated and extended the building as a care home and a girls' school, called 'Holy Angels' and in time, built on a chapel.

Although the houses are protected structures, the land is destined for development. Two privately-owned walkways span the road and link the properties. One walkway made of wrought iron is reached by means of a spiral stairway. The other enclosed bridge replaced an earlier walkway that was damaged by a truck. Following rejection of an appeal to An Bord Pleanala, permission has been granted for the removal of both bridges.

The entrance portico to Glenmaroon House. Courtesy REA Coonan (Maynooth) WK Nowlan Property.

View of Guinness family home, Glenmaroon and the covered walkway, looking down Knockmaroon Hill. Courtesy Reynolds Family Private Collection.

Tony Reynolds

Knockmaroon Hill is steep for cyclists who have to dismount and push their bikes uphill and a challenge to anybody who chooses to cycle downhill. One cold morning, I was heading down Knockmaroon hill in my old Vauxhall with my brother-in-law, John, in the passenger seat. There was no indication at all that the roads were icy until we started down the steep hill and realised it was like a sheet of glass. The car was wavering but I couldn't brake. I tried to steer gently but the car crashed into the wall opposite, then it veered into a high doorstep that protruded into the road and spun around twice. Amazingly, the car was still going after all that. *'Are you alright?'* I said to John, *'Yes, you?'* he replied. *'Let's get out of here, so.'* With that, we shot off to Chapelizod and pulled into Syms Garage at Maiden's Row – I knew the mechanic - to take stock of the damage. The chrome was dented and the radiator was leaking but a bit of Radweld fixed that – it was marvellous stuff.

The Brass Castle, the Officer's Headquarters of the Royal Irish Artillery regiment, once stood near the foot of Knockmaroon Hill. In my time, P. Joe Glynn was a bit of a character who lived at the Brass Castle. He used to deliver telegrams for the Post Office and run errands for the Guards. The Guards' Barracks was once located beside the Mullingar House pub and when it was re-located, the Lions Club used the building.

Cissy and Lily Thewlis lived in a house at the bottom of Knockmaroon Hill when I was growing up. The Thewlis sisters were prominent members of Cumann na mBan, and nieces of Agnes and Michael Mallin, latter who was executed in 1916. Cissy worked in Castleknock College.

Knockmaroon Hill, looking up towards footbridge and Glenmaroon staff quarters. Courtesy Daniel O'Neill, Panoramio.

13.
HALLOWEEN AND CHRISTMAS

At Halloween, we played games such as 'bobbing apple,' where you bit an apple while it bobbed in a basin of water or 'snap apple,' where you had to bite an apple dangling on a string - good luck to you if the apple was swinging. As darkness approached, children dressed in old clothes and put on face masks, held on by elastic string – 'false faces', we called them. The garb was much less elaborate than nowadays – children improvised, often using the same masks each year.

Groups of us children called to different houses in the neighbourhood. '*Any apples or nuts,*' we'd say, once the door opened. We never shouted out, '*trick-or-treat,*' which is American. Some households had a reputation for being generous, so needless to say they were our first targets. Knockmaroon House, home to the Guinness family of Lord Moyne, was top of the list. They used to bring us into the sitting room and get us to sing a song in Irish for their children. Well aware we'd get a box of sweets, like the type we sold in the shop, we used to sing for Ireland. Lord Moyne had a large family with his second wife and I remember some of the children wearing kilts. Uniformed nursemaids used to wheel the children out in high prams, often to the Phoenix Park.

Later on, it was time for fireworks which were perfectly legal and in plentiful supply. We sold some in our shop, as did Molloy's shop in Castleknock. However, if you wanted impressive ones, town was the best place to go. As well as *bangers, squibs, rockets, Roman Candles* and *Catherine wheels*, there were *nine-hoppers*, also called *'gutter bullies'* which exploded and jumped indiscriminately nine times, terrorising everybody in their path. Castleknock College held firework displays on top of Tower hill, up beside the water tank.

Christmas in the 1940s. The smell of nutmeg, cinnamon and cloves and extra stock in the shop - dried fruit, raisins, currants, sultanas, almond paste and Royal icing for the Christmas cake and pudding. As Christmas approached, the smell of whiskey being poured on the cake again and again. The real build-up to the festive season started around Our Lady's Feast Day on 8th of December, when people from the country traditionally came to the city to shop.

We were among the luckier children brought each year to meet Santa who was invariably ensconced in a decorated grotto or cavern-like corridor in large Department Stores such as Clery's in O'Connell Street, Switzer's in Grafton Street, or Pim's in George's Street. The city streets were festooned with Christmas lights and jingles played alongside carol singers in full swing. Children wrote to Santa in politer-than-usual terms, listing the presents they hoped to receive. The house was decorated with sprigs of holly and colourful paper-chain decorations; I never remember mistletoe at all. Everybody in the locality was accustomed to frequenting Guinness's wood to collect sticks for the fire but coming up to Christmas, they chopped down a small coniferous tree. The Christmas tree decorations were hauled out once they got the tree home.

Castleknock – Memories of a Neighbourhood

The excitement reached its peak on Christmas Eve, with the expectation of a visit down the chimney from the great man himself and more importantly, the toys he brought. A glass of whiskey and a piece of cake were left beside the fireplace alongside carrots for Rudolph. Another Christmas treat was a trip into town to see a pantomime, usually in The Queen's Theatre, The Theatre Royal or The Olympia. Getting together with cousins and paying visits over the school holidays made it all the more exciting.

My mother was up and out to early Mass in the College Chapel on Christmas morning and home sharp to put on the turkey. The kitchen steamed up with the smell of the turkey as my mother timed the cooking by the pound. Meanwhile, we were enjoying Santa's gifts, usually dolls and prams for the girls and guns, cowboy outfits and cars for the boys as well as books, games, and annuals. One of my best presents was a cinematograph which worked off electric light and showed 'still' films on the wall. Over the years, I also got model cars, toy soldiers, trains on tracks and bicycles. Other children were not so lucky – I know of some who got an orange in their Christmas stocking and others who never heard of Santa at all.

After Mass at Porterstown Chapel, it was back home to a fry-up – sausages, rashers, black and white pudding, egg and sometimes tomatoes and mushrooms, depending on the taste buds. The table was set with shiny cutlery and the best table cloth, napkins and delph. We wore paper hats and pulled crackers. We stuck to traditional Christmas food - stuffed turkey, ham, spiced beef, roast potatoes, brussel sprouts, carrots, parsnips and all the usual trimmings. A sprig of holly decorated the pudding and when the time was right, my father poured whiskey on top and set it alight. After lunch, we played cards as well as board games such as *Ludo and Snakes and Ladders*. In the evening, we tucked into Christmas cake and mince pies. We always had visitors on Christmas Day – Aunt Jen came over from Ashtown with her husband, Ned, their friend, Neddy Breaney, a cobbler from Donabate, and Joe Lyng. I lost touch with Joe Lyng, but I heard that he emigrated to Canada and became a water inspector.

Our range became unreliable at a stage when I had a car, so I used to drive over to my Aunt Fanny's in Rathgar with the turkey and call back on Christmas Eve to collect the cooked turkey.

On Stephen's Day, the Wren Boys used to call house-to-house, dressed garishly. At one time, the tradition was to carry a wren in a small box singing laments for the unfortunate bird and look to raise money for the funeral. The Wren Boys who called to us never had a bird with them - they were usually from outside the area, often school boys on bikes. Older guys were after money for a few drinks in the pub. They used to sing a ditty, usually accompanied by the mouth organ or melodian. We gave them a cash tip, bananas or apples. This old Irish custom has almost died out - it is still kept alive in some areas, such as Dingle and Sandymount.

"The wren, the wren, the king of all birds,
On St. Stephen's Day was caught in the furze;
Up with the kettle and down with the pan,
Pray give us a penny to bury the wran."

(Traditional Irish Wren song)

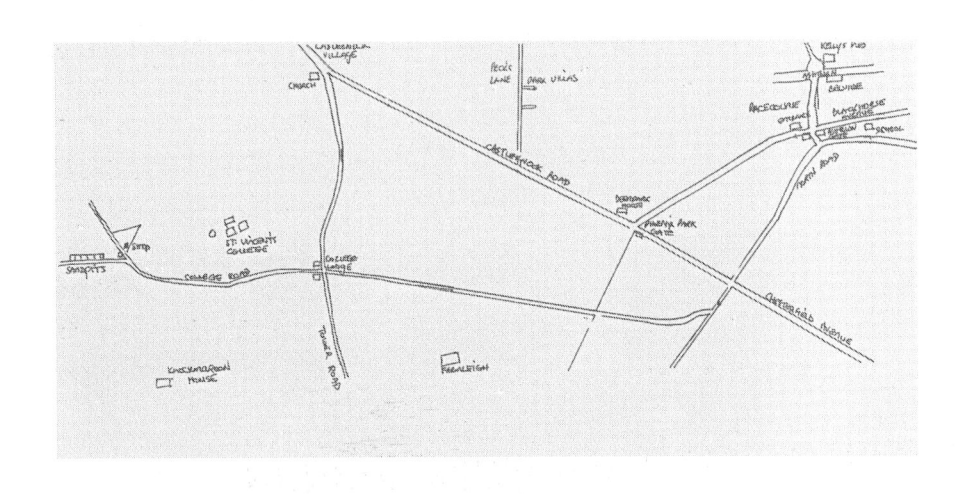

14.
THE RACECOURSE NEWSPAPER RUN

The 'racecourse' newspaper round was always done by Christy ('Kit') Lawless, employed by my father, but if for some reason Kit couldn't do it, I'd step into the breach after school. This involved cycling to Castleknock village and on towards town. A large house covered in Virginia creeper once stood on the town side of the garage, with its back to the road. A chap I knew, Michael Greene, lived there until the family moved nearer to town. Coincidentally, when they moved out, another family called Greene moved in. Mrs. Greene lived there for years with her daughter who worked as a medic in Blanchardstown hospital. The house was demolished in the 1980s to make way for the Castleknock Village Centre. Across the road was the one pub in Castleknock, McKenna's, later 'Myo's.'

Oak Cottage. Courtesy Reynolds Family Private Collection.

Castleknock – Memories of a Neighbourhood

A little further on towards town are 'Oak Lodge,' a dormer bungalow, 'Lisnagree,' and next is 'Beech Lodge,' once the gate lodge to a driveway leading up to an imposing house, 'Castleknock Lodge.'

Next came the dispensary which is still there, located opposite the traffic light junction with Auburn Avenue. Dr. Cullen used to live in the doctor's residence behind the dispensary and later on, Dr Lavelle. His practice covered an area extending as far as Porterstown and Clonsilla. Many a time I was sent on my bike for Dr. Cullen who used to pay house visits. The other local doctor, Dr. Merrick, lived at Fawn Lodge opposite the Castleknock Park gate. The doctors were available 24/7 back then and house visits by car were commonplace. There was no such thing as having to make an appointment with the doctor.

Beech Lodge. Courtesy Reynolds Family Private Collection.

Castleknock Dispensary – Ardnagreine, Castleknock, Co. Dublin. Photo courtesy Dr. Mark Humphreys, papers of Patricia Lavelle.

The Hoyles lived in a bungalow beside the dispensary. Mr. Hoyle worked for the local County Council as a supervisor over the roads. He wore a suit and hat and he rode a bicycle. The Hoyles had a son, Aidan, was in school with me. In 1938, the rector moved from Mount Hybla on White's Road, into a house called 'Elm Grove,' beside the dispensary. When my father died, I went to the rector to fix up a grave in the cemetery and he referred me on to Mr. Higgins, the sexton who lived opposite the Protestant church in Castleknock.

At the corner of Castleknock Road and Peck's Lane. Hannah Phelan lived in a two-storey double-fronted house with fields behind it. The name 'Peck' derived from a military man, Colonel Peck, who once lived along the lane. What I particularly remember from my childhood is the stuffed squirrel she had on the window ledge over the front door. Nearby, the Clarke family lived for a while in a cottage with its gable end to the road.

Park Villas comprised several rows of artisan houses built along Peck's Lane in the 1920s for ex-British soldiers. The houses have a distinctive dormer style with a red lattice pattern roof. They usually had four rooms and a scullery, with a front garden and generous rear gardens, for growing vegetables. These ex-army houses were built in small pockets countrywide, usually in blocks of four or six in urban areas and either semi-detached or detached in rural areas. This housing

Park Villas Peck's Lane. The last house to develop its garden site, now cleared for development. Courtesy Reynolds Family Private Collection.

stock was managed by a Trust until the 1950s, when they were offered for sale to the tenants. These ex-army style houses are still recognisable today, despite extensions and alterations. All the gardens at Park Villas now accommodate new houses, bar one last house currently undergoing development.

One of my uncles, Tommy Reilly, an ex-British soldier, lived in Park Villas with his wife, Maggie, and my cousins - Tom, Fanny, Peg, Jen, Agnes, Sadie, May, Josie and Nell. The girls were much sought after at local dances. Another uncle, Peter Reynolds, also an ex-British soldier, lived in Park Villas with his wife and my cousins, Tommy, Peter, Kathleen, Peggy and Nora. My uncle Peter had been gassed in the trenches in Arras, France during WWI. Afterwards, he got a job in the Civil Service where he rose through the ranks. Peggy Reynolds and May Reilly were close friends – they were both cousins of mine but were not related.

A large number of families lived in Park Villas. Some who come to mind are the Forans, the Dempseys, the Purcells, the Byrnes, the Walkers, the Caseleys, the Kellys, the Hills, the Spaines and the Christians. Many of the children from Peck's Lane were at school in Castleknock - some made contributions to the already mentioned Schools Folklore Collection. My father's best man was Jimmy Christian, originally from Blackhorse Lane, as we called it. Jimmy moved to Peck's Lane after he married. Jimmy's son, Tommy Christian, was a friend of mine from the scouts and went to my school. When I was about fourteen, one of Tommy's sisters arrived over at my house on her bike with a jumper she had knitted. I presumed she had knit it for Tommy and it didn't fit. Across the lane, Jack Fagan, the local meter reader, lived in a bungalow that backed on to fields. He went about his business on a bike, with a thick ledger strapped to the rear carrier. At the far end of Peck's Lane just at the Navan Road junction was the Seagraves imposing farm house. Tessa Seagrave, who had a head of curly hair, was in school with me. Our neighbour, Mickey Harford, was also brought up in Peck's Lane.

Back to the junction of Peck's Lane and the Castleknock Road. Up to the 1970s, from here to the Phoenix Park gate was all fields. There was no Georgian Village or "Millionaires Row," (as it was nicknamed) much less Stockton, Auburn Avenue, Oaklodge, Oakview, Castleknock Park, Castleknock Pines, Hadleigh and so forth.

A Mr. Bishop lived in a house that backed on to the wall of the Phoenix Park, right beside the Castleknock Park gate. A former politician, Michael Keating, later lived there. Some newer houses built along this laneway used to have a stable or two behind, handy for a canter in the Park.

Deerpark House. Courtesy Reynolds Family Private Collection.

Deerpark House sits opposite the Castleknock gate of the Phoenix Park - its gate pillars are topped with a stag's head. This was home to an English couple, Mr. and Mrs. Sykes - it was said that Mr. Sykes had been a tea planter in India. He used a huge basket chair on four wheels drawn by a pony to get about; his wife walked beside him. Deerpark House was sold on to Christy Grassick, who bred and trained racehorses. An entrance to the side of the house led into a stable yard.

Dr. Merrick, who was formerly a British Army doctor, lived in 'Fawn Lodge,' the house beside Grassicks. The apartment block now built there carries the name.

Photograph of Phoenix Park Gate Lodge, Castleknock.

Castleknock – Memories of a Neighbourhood

Travelling from Deerpark House towards the racecourse, a row of two storey houses faced the wall of the Phoenix Park. The 'Jubilee' nurse lived in one of those houses. In fact, she was the District midwife who worked with the doctors in the community and cycled all over the district with her Gladstone bag, doing home visits. Anybody who needed dressings was referred by the doctor to the Jubilee nurse - her clinic was based at the dispensary in Castleknock. The nurse eventually moved to the row of houses built alongside the Half Way House in Ashtown.

After the row of houses was Mahady's cottage and then, Mackeys Garden Centre. I remember passing by these cottages after a heavy rainfall and some of the inhabitants bailing water out of their houses. Next to the garden centre was the entrance gate to the horse racing yard of 'The Rasher' Byrne, who was always known by this nickname. He was married to Dr. Cullen's daughter and he was a brother of Mickey Byrne, who trained horses at the bottom of the lane beyond O'Hely's cottage. 'The Rasher' was a shrewd man who was known to plan winning strategies for his racehorses.

W. J. 'Rasher' Byrne trained in the Phoenix Park, specialising in handicap coups, viz: Splendour (1946 Irish Cambridgeshire) and Abeltai (1964 Irish Cesarewitch). Rare overseas ventures yielded Royal Ascot success with Marshall Ney (1954 Jersey Stakes) and Abeltai (1965 Newbury Autumn Cup). Courtesy Irish Racehorse Trainer's Association (IRTA).

In the 1970s, Deerpark estate was built behind Deerpark House and it covered a large area, extending as far as the Phoenix Park racecourse. On the perimeter of this estate, Park View replaced the row of houses facing the wall of the Phoenix Park, Mahady's cottage and the Rasher Byrne's. This stretch of road always had a problem with flooding drains, even when the late politician, Brian Lenihan Senior, lived at Park View. The garden centre is gone now and in its place are the Chesterfield and Castleknock Gate developments.

Opposite the boundary wall of the Park, the Phoenix Park racecourse extended to 175 acres and had both six furlong and seven furlong courses. Originally, the course was used for steeplechasing and hurdles but later on, it was used solely for flat racing. The founding members of the racecourse which opened in 1902 were Sir John Arnott, Harry Peard and Major Loder. The Manager of the Phoenix Park racecourse in my time was Harry Peard, a huge man who lived in a large

Tudor style house on the grounds. The house backed against the perimeter wall and overlooked the Ashtown roundabout. Harry's wife took over when he died. Our shop delivered a daily newspaper to Mr. Peard. I remember going in their gate and down a tree-lined driveway and he'd be out at the door waiting on his paper. *"Where's 'Lightening' today?"* he used to say, on seeing me instead of Kit. This was his sarcastic name for Kit Lawless who used to ride a bicycle so slowly, you'd think it was going to topple over. Sir John Arnott then took over. He was a brother of Maxwell Arnott, a gentleman horse trainer with stables in Clonsilla.

One time home of Harry Peard and the Arnott family. Courtesy Jim Lacey, historian and author, Blanchardstown-Castleknock Historical Society.

Evening meetings at the race-course brought the after-work crowd from town. Cars used to be parked up on the kerbs along the Navan Road and the Castleknock Road and on the grass inside the Ashtown Park gate.

Later on, an entertainment complex was built on the race-course. As well as a restaurant, it comprised 'Silks' nightclub, the Squash Ireland sports complex and function rooms at which many a local wedding and party were held.

Once the writing was on the wall for the racecourse, the two Phoenix statues that stood majestically above the entrance gate to the racecourse disappeared. A Tudor style kiosk, white-washed with black timbers and a red tiled roof, unfortunately burned down. At one time, planning permission was sought for a casino on the racecourse but local opposition put paid to that plan. Apartment blocks now occupy the racecourse site.

A manor house called Belleville stood opposite the entrance to the racecourse. Painted black and white, it backed onto the Navan Road at Ashtown. Mrs. Marion Hendron owned Belleville - the Hendrons ran a hardware and fuels business in the city centre. A girl nicknamed "Gypsy" McGrath lived at Belleville.

Belleville, Ashtown, adjacent to Phoenix Park. Courtesy Reynolds Family Private Collection.

Blackhorse Riding School operated from at Belleville's stable block beside the gate lodge at the top of Blackhorse Avenue. There used to be a 'mounting block' here, right at the road's edge. This stable block gained notoriety when the Head of the Irish National Building Society, Jim Lacey, was kidnapped and held there. Belleville has since been developed as a housing estate bearing the same name. Beside it, there is another estate appropriately called The Paddocks.

The Ashtown gate into the Phoenix Park is directly across the road from the entrances to Belleville and the racecourse. The gatekeeper's lodge is to the left of the gate. In my mother's time, the building on the right was an RIC barracks known as Bessborough Barracks. This building now provides housing for park staff.

Former Bessborough Barracks at Ashtown Gate, Phoenix Park, 2017. Courtesy Reynolds Family Private Collection.

Beyond the barracks was the Park Superintendent's Home, Park Lodge, which backs onto the park wall, opposite the racecourse. Mr Ennis lived there with his wife and two daughters, noted beauties, who attracted glances when they got on the bus.

Aerial view of Ashtown showing Belleville (bottom right), Kelly's Pub (on the right above Belleville), Ashtown Tinbox Factory (on the left above Belleville) and the road leading down to the railway.

Here's a photo of Ashtown Crossroads c. 1948. In the centre of the photograph, you can identify the Ashtown Tin Box company, where DG Gowan are

Above left: Horse-riding advertisement in Trinity College News 1966. Courtesy Trinity College. Below left: St Vincent's Navan Road. Courtesy Sisters of Charity, St. Vincent's, Navan Road. Right: My sister Maureen and myself at the pump, Reilly family home on the Navan Road. Courtesy Reynolds Family Private Collection.

now located. To the right is the monument to Martin Savage, which was relocated from the roundabout to the wall of the race-course. On the far right in the photograph is Kelly's Pub – the Halfway House. In the far background is the dome of Dunsink Observatory and in the foreground, you can see Belleville. At one time, training stables and farms dominated the landscape from the Phoenix Park all the way to Clonee and spreading outwards towards Dunsink and they gave great employment.

My mother's family, the Reillys, lived in a cottage right opposite the entrance to St. Vincent's on the Navan Road, an institution established by the Daughters of Charity. My mother's sister, Aunt Jen, lived on there with her husband, Ned. Aunt Jen was like a second mother to us. When our mother was hospitalised with pneumonia a few times, Aunt Jen came to look after us. The Reillys attended the Park School – it closed as a national school in the 1960s. The President and Phoenix Park residents still cast their votes at that school when there is a General Election or Referendum.

Beside the school, there's a turreted cottage, known as the 'concrete' cottage, because mass concrete was used in its construction.

National School, Phoenix Park, attended by my mother. Courtesy Reynolds Family Private Collection.

'Concrete' Cottage, Phoenix Park. (Also, the plantation I used for shelter when faced with an oncoming plane, attempting to land). Courtesy Reynolds Family Private Collection.

Eye witness account:

In 1919, during the early stages of the Irish War of Independence, my mother witnessed an historic moment. It was the attempted assassination of the British Lord Lieutenant, Lord French, at Ashtown, as he made his way back from his estate in Frenchpark, Roscommon, to the Vice-regal Lodge in the Phoenix Park. After her lunch break, my mother was returning to work at the shoe polish factory at Ashtown Mill, adjacent to the Royal Canal. When she got near to Kelly's pub, she heard gun shots, so she held back and hid.

As Lord French's party left the train station, some I.R.A. men pushed a farm cart across the road to block the entourage and they fired shots with handguns. However, the cart had left a gap so Lord French was able to speed on to safety through the gap and the ambush failed. Martin Savage was shot in the neck and Dan Breen was shot in the ankle.

Once the commotion had died down, my mother saw men coming out with bicycles from behind the entrance to St. Patrick's Home along the Navan Road. As the men started cycling towards town, she noticed that one man had no bike – he was kneeling on the carrier at the back of a bike and had a

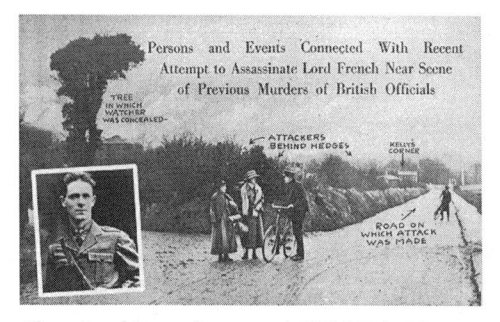

Photo of road from railway towards Kelly's Pub, Ashtown – route taken by Lord French before ambush attempt. Accessed from An Poblacht website, courtesy of unknown photographer.

foot injury. My mother headed back to work, past the crowd that was milling beside Kelly's pub. A crowd had surrounded a man and carried him to the door of the pub, but they were not admitted. Then a crowd of British soldiers arrived in trucks and started to search the surrounding fields, but none of them thought of searching for the assailants in the direction of town and nobody informed them, so the assailants got away.

My mother later read in the newspaper that to blend in, the I.R.A. men had played handball in the handball alley* behind the Halfway House. It was

---

* Back then, handball alleys adjacent to pubs were commonplace, e.g. the Ball Alley pub in Lucan.

Dan Breen that had gone past her on the back of a bike with an injured foot. He was smuggled into the Mater Hospital for treatment to his wound and sneaked out later. Dan Breen survived another gunshot wound in a different incident. It was Martin Savage who had been surrounded by a crowd at Kelly's pub, but he had died. There's a statue to Martin Savage at this point in Ashtown.

15.
THE WAR YEARS

As World War II started when I was twelve, I remember those years well. Although Ireland was neutral, precautions still had to be taken to combat the difficulties with imports and exports and the danger of attack, so the Government brought in certain measures during this period, which was known as 'The Emergency.'

There was a scurry to listen to news bulletins on the radio and everybody was obliged to keep lights off at night and employ 'blackout' curtains to cover the windows, as lights were liable to attract attention from stray bomber planes. At one stage, bombs were dropped at the North Strand and in the Phoenix Park. Newsreels shown before films in cinemas kept people abreast of the happenings.

Turf banks in the Phoenix Park during WWII.

Tony Reynolds

During the Emergency, The Turf Board, now Bord na Mona, was established to organise the cutting of turf on the midland bogs and have it transported to the cities and towns. Thousands of tons of turf were transported to Dublin and stored in high mounds of up to thirty feet, along the main road of the Phoenix Park and on the Fifteen Acres. In addition, wire bales and timber bollards, side-by-side and up to roof height, were placed at intervals of about 200 yards, to prevent planes using the road as a runway. As cyclists could not get by, a few of them used to get together and move the bollards, leaving gaps so that cyclists could at least dismount and negotiate around the turf banks. Every now and then, the powers-that-be dragged them in close again. For the duration of the Emergency, this performance went on of alternate gaps-no gaps.

A concrete machine gun nest was constructed on the grass beside Mountjoy corner which was mostly at subterranean level. At above ground level, small slits at intervals in the concrete construction were intended as firing points.

Another measure taken during the Emergency was along the Tower Road, which runs from the College Lodge towards Knockmaroon Hill. Two huge concrete bollards, over four feet in height, were placed on either side of the road, to deliberately narrow it. Two holes, one over the other, were left in each bollard. The bore of the holes was designed to fit old railway sleepers and indeed, several railway sleepers lay idle on the grassy bank, ready for action. The idea was that in the event of invasion, the sleepers could be quickly inserted into the holes to prevent through traffic. The Tower Road has not changed at all in my lifetime - bordered by a path on one side and a bank on the other, it is still the same width.

As the airfield between Coolmine and Porterstown was eminently suitable for aircraft to land, the field was spiked with sleepers during the war. Nevertheless, I remember a sputtering plane overhead one day, with its engine cutting out and the odd bang. I knew it was headed towards the airfield so I got on my bike and headed to Porterstown. By the time I reached the airfield, the plane had crashed-landed. In the course of landing, the plane had ploughed through the tall hedge between the airfield and the windmill field. Its nose was stuck in the ground and its tail was in the air. An Irish army officer and another man were strolling around the field. A few hours later, an Air Corps tow truck arrived on the scene. I was amazed to see them hacking off the wings with hammers, bars and hacksaws before raising the body of the plane onto their tow truck. For about two years after that, there was a gap in the hedge.

Another afternoon, at about 2.30 p.m., I was cycling home along the North Road of the Phoenix Park , near to the Hole-in-the-Wall pub, when I encountered an oncoming plane fast approaching me. It was only about ten feet above the ground, obviously attempting a landing. I quickly dismounted and dragged my bicycle to one side. The plane careered up high. It was a spitfire with RAF circles under its wings and its engine was backfiring. When it circled, I knew it was going to attempt another landing, so this time, I crossed the road to a plantation, propped the bicycle against the railings, climbed over and lay low. The plane failed to land a second time and sputtered as it began circling again. I was listening for a bang, but when there was none, I gathered it had landed. Guessing it had landed on the racecourse, I pedalled like hell to watch the action. I steadied my bike against the sleepers of the perimeter fence and stood on the saddle to peer over, but I could see nothing. Afterwards, I read in the paper that after landing on the racecourse, the pilot had started burning papers. The military had orders to destroy documents and maps for security reasons, if under threat of capture. The pilot was interrupted by the Racecourse Manager, the formidable Mrs. Peard, who headed up the gun club that operated at the racecourse. Mysteriously, the plane found its way back to England within a few weeks.

Standard issue gas masks

As Ireland was neutral, prisoners-of-war were held at the Curragh Camp in Kildare, where the custody rules allowed them to attend local dances. Some of those incarcerated met and married Irish girls. Many prisoners-of-war did not want their detention to end, for fear of being repatriated and quickly returned to the front. The film, 'The Brylcreem Boys,' shows prisoners-of-war at the Curragh getting into scrapes with their enemies behind bars.

During the war, the Government distributed gas masks to everybody. You had to try them on to ensure they fitted, but they were awfully claustrophobic and left you gasping for breath. Our initials were printed on the square brown boxes that contained our masks. For the duration of the war, our gas masks hung under the stairs on long cords, ready for use. Years later, the gas masks were still in our coal house gathering dust.

The Government were in constant fear of invasion during World War II, so they kept the Irish army trained up by organising military manoeuvres from time to time. In 1941, one such review took place that lasted about two or three weeks, involving one army group advancing towards Dublin, pitted against another army group in defence. Farmers kicked up holy war because some of the army trucks were crossing their land.

A whole bunch of soldiers ended up milling about near our shop. Us young lads were transfixed watching these soldiers - carrying real guns - hopping down from trucks and going in and out of our shop. When my sister, Maureen, appeared with a camera, some of the soldiers lent myself and my younger brother Noel their .303 guns and tin hats so we could have our photo taken. Here we are with our favourite dog, Trixie.

Tony & Noel Reynolds with borrowed tin hats and guns, and Trixie. Courtesy Reynolds Family Private Collection.

Many young men from the area joined the British Army, including Billy Clarke from Clonsilla, who was an easy-going fellow. Billy was one of those who crossed the Channel on D-Day in 1944 and ended up on the Normandy beaches. He told me afterwards that with fire coming at them from front and behind, the sounds around him were deafening. He thought he'd never be able to hear right again. Billy said there was debris

Photograph of Billy Clarke.

all around in the water, bits from explosions and dead bodies floating by and if you fell in, you mightn't get up again.

When Billy Clarke served in Burma later on, everybody waited for news of him. Any time there were reports of heavy fighting there, people presumed Billy was involved and used to remark, *'Billy Clarke is in the middle of all that.'* After the war in Burma, Billy told me that he never even heard a shot in Burma; the only enemy he saw were a few 'Japs,' prisoners-of-war, going by on the back of a truck. He was four days in a troop train all across India and every time the train stopped, there were beggars pleading for alms. After the war, Billy spent time in Australia and New Zealand. Those who signed up were seen as heroes to us young lads, who indulged in role play, always on the winning side, of course!

England were refused the use of Irish ports due to Ireland's neutrality, so they remained hostile and disinclined to trade. Nevertheless, Ireland exported milk and meat to England and they sent across coal, but it was the lowest grade of coal, called 'slack.' Slack was difficult to burn and gave out little heat - sometimes it had to be mixed with timber and turf. Inchicore Works built a bricketting plant where the slack was compressed with the addition of a type of concrete 'dusting' into usable fuel briquettes.

All fuel was rationed: petrol, paraffin oil and gas. With the scarcity of fuel, public transport services declined - train services and bus services were delayed or curtailed. Cars belonging to the priest, the doctor, and taxis were considered 'essential' but even then, they had to operate on limited petrol supplies. It meant most people were on bikes again, and the pony and trap and the horse and cart were back in vogue as modes of transport.

Dr. Horgan, who lived in Castleknock village, had a gas contraption fitted to the roof of his car at the start of World War II. As a doctor of science, he had some involvement with this new-fangled invention which was used not alone in Ireland, but in England too. A number of vans used to go around, delivering the fuel supply. It looked like a massive balloon fastened to the roof that stretched the full length of the car. The door of the boot was removed and the boot itself was used as a receptacle for two upright gas cyclinders that supplied the car with fuel - one of them was an open fire fuelled by coke. The car smoked as it went along the road, its huge balloon swaying. In 1940, a new Government Order banned these gas contraptions and confined fuel supplies even further.

During the war, my father brought me into town and bought me a brand new

Raleigh bicycle. It was almost impossible to buy a tube or a tyre for a bicycle, so many tried out ingenious ideas, such as lining the tyre with strips of canvas or stuffing them with hay. A man who lived in Clonsilla and worked on the docks was able to procure bicycle tyres on the black market - sailors brought them from the continent. The price was way over the odds, up to a pound. We used to nab him as he cycled past the shop to put in our orders.

Ration Cards were introduced for every citizen to share out essential commodities such as tea, coffee, sugar, clothes and other items. The 'card' specified the entitlements and customers came to the shop on a weekly basis for their 'rations'. The tea ration was one ounce per person per week; sugar was eight ounces and butter was six ounces. The rationed items had to be carefully weighed into brown bags and labelled with the customer's name. One customer always argued about her rations and threatened to report Peter Reynolds to Mr. Lemass – we called her 'Thunder and Lightning'. As shop owners, we had more than most people – a square box in our parlour held a secret stash of tea, kept strictly for special occasions, policed by my mother. My elderly aunt used to wake up on occasion and call out, 'hide the tea caddy'. During the war, the Irish sung a version of Vera Lynn's sweethearts' song 'Bless Them All':

Extract of Government Order, 1942 – rationing of soap. Courtesy of Oireachtas website.

> *Bless 'em all. Bless 'em all.*
> *The long and the short and the tall,*
> *Bless De Valera and Seán McEntee,*
> *They gave us the black flour,*
> *And the half-ounce of tea.*

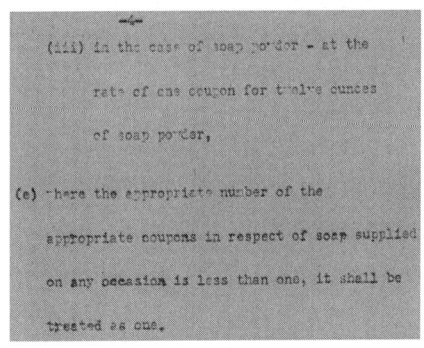

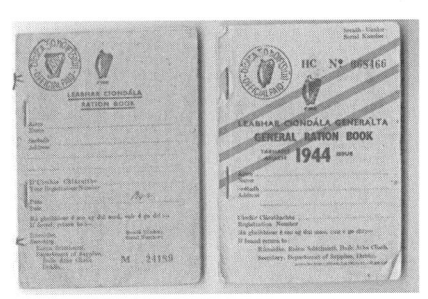

Typical Ration Book. Courtesy of Oireachtas website.

Clothing and footwear were strictly rationed so if you wanted to look smart, you had to adopt various strategies. Shoes and boots were re-soled and the uppers were patched. Tailors 'turned' suits by unpicking the seams and re-stitching the garment with the unworn side of the material out. Shirts were patched and the collars were 'turned.' Coupons were often 'pooled' to buy items for special occasions. In particular, nylon stockings were prized, so women were vigilant to avoid snagging. Any snags elicited curses from even the most ladylike, who were obliged to mend the ladder with the finest of needles and catgut thread. As nylons generally had a single seam up the back, some ladies took to using a colour on their bare legs and drawing a vertical line as a 'pretend' seam from the heel up along the calf to mimic seamed stockings.

Due to the shortage of imports, land in the Phoenix Park was leased to Dublin Corporation for use as allotments. The Government imposed compulsory tillage for farmers as no grain was being imported. Every farmer was obliged to make the best use of any land and sow a certain acreage of wheat, at risk of prosecution for non-compliance. The Compulsory Tillage Order was policed by Government Inspectors. A severe outbreak of Foot and Mouth in March 1941 spread over much of the country – over 550 farms had outbreaks and thousands of animals had to be slaughtered. It took months before it was finally eradicated.

As any landed estates lying idle had to be sublet, Mr. Malone who farmed up the Coolmine Road, rented land at Leixlip Castle and beside Mulhuddart graveyard. The castle figured largely in my life over the war years, seeing as I was friendly with all the Malones, especially Paddy and John, who were of an age with me. They told me it was a killer trying to plough at Leixlip Castle, as the fields had not been ploughed for years. The plough kept stumbling on massive tree roots and stones for twenty feet inside the hedges. In order to keep all the land tilled and sown with crops, the tractor was going twenty-four hours at the busiest times. The lads had to chip in; they often stayed up all night long to keep things running, with the aid of lamps. In addition to compulsory tillage for landowners, people cultivated the smallest of patches. Even front gardens were dug to grow potatoes, vegetables and fruit.

Prices of all essentials were controlled. Wages and salaries were also controlled and any increases were Government-sanctioned. As there were few imports, we had to rely on Irish wheat for bread-making. Only then did people realised the extent of our reliance on imported wheat. Bread made from Irish wheat was dirty white in colour, stodgy and lumpy too – you often had to pick the lumps out. It was very unpalatable and hard to get it down without butter and jam to add a bit of taste.

Although World War I was before my time, a sadness enveloped our family when I was growing up. An uncle of mine, Philip Reilly, aged sixteen, had used an older brother's birth certificate to sign up, without telling anyone. Philip was my mother's younger brother. My Granny got a letter from Philip who was stationed in a training camp at Maryborough, Queen's County, now known as Portlaoise. He may have had romantic notions, given the army service of his older brother, Tommy, but some said he had signed up in fear, having been reported for trespassing on farmland and cautioned by the Guards. Then my Granny got another letter from Philip to say he was leaving for France with his regiment.

World War I was into its fourth week when Philip was killed at the Battle of the Marne, just gone seventeen. His older brother, Tommy Reilly, found Philip's body. Tommy was already in France and had no idea that Philip had joined up. My Granny and the rest of the family took comfort in knowing that Tommy had buried Philip.

After the war, Tommy got a job at the Post Office in James's Street and he worked there until retirement. A long time after Philip's mother and siblings had died, Tommy's daughter, Josie, told me that her father had eventually come clean about Philip. Although Tommy had indeed found Philip's body, he could not bury him because he was not on burial detail and had other duties. Philip is one of the few of his regiment whose body was identified and thus, his name is on his grave in France.

Above and top right: Photograph of letter from Philip Reilly to his mother. Courtesy Reynolds Private Family Collection.

Castleknock – Memories of a Neighbourhood

> 3 Tell the baba I was asking for her I was looking out for her when we were going. down we past the place We went that evening in the five to four train and we were in Marbourgugh station at six o'clock and we had to carry our kits with us. I don't know when we will be finished but I think we will be breking up on the tenth of the next month I am not a bit lonely down here I am in the band plaing a drum and I do get it easy all we have to do is to shoot every day no more at present
>
> I remain Dear Mother Your fond brother Philip

DEBT OF HONOUR REGISTER

In Memory of

P REILLY

Private
10931
2nd Bn., Connaught Rangers

who died on
Monday 14 September 1914

VAILLY BRITISH CEMETERY Aisne, France
Sp. Mem. 7.

Above: Registry entry, Commonwealth War Graves Commission. (CWGC). Record of Philip Reilly's service, 1914. Courtesy Reynolds Family Private Collection.

Left: Photograph of my Uncle, Philip Reilly, who died in the fourth week of WWI, 1914. Courtesy Reynolds Private Family Collection.

16.
HUNTING AND GROWN UP PURSUITS

Growing up in the 1930s and 1940s, our neighbourhood teemed with birds and their distinctive sounds were in the air - cawing crows, cooing pigeons, chattering magpies, the cuckoo in spring and corncrakes in Captain Steed's fields. Singing birds were plentiful too - thrushes, blackbirds, linnets and more, not to mention all the small birds - swallows, sparrows, robins and wrens. Although some are relatively rare in Ireland now, where has the rest of the population gone? The colourful birds are gone missing too - yellow hammers, jays, finches and the barn owl glowing in the night. Wildlife was more abundant too — hedgehogs, badgers, foxes, even mink. Back then, red squirrels were more commonly seen — now, you only see grey squirrels.

Myself and Tommy Fox from Orchard Terrace were keen on collecting birds eggs, although his cache was bigger than mine. We collected every type from sparrows to robins, wrens and tits and marsh-dwellers such as plovers. We were always on the lookout for new varieties and we had the gathering process down to an art form. Generally, eggs laid by smaller birds were easier to access while the parent birds were away from the nest - an egg each could be easily removed without repercussions. Bigger birds built in more inaccessible places and the nest was often abandoned if disturbed. Magpies are inclined to build in the middle of a blackthorn bush and crows build high in the trees. To preserve the eggs, you made a pin prick hole in the shell and blew out the yolk and the white, leaving just the shell. I kept my egg collection in a box secreted away in the far shed behind the shop.

Before the time of the combine harvester, farmers used a reaper and binder. They cut the grain, wrapped it into sheaves and propped the sheaves upright into stucks, heads down, to let them dry over the following weeks. The stucks were brought to the mill where the grain was taken off, leaving only the straw. As reaping deprived mice and rats of their homes, the field creatures raced in under the stucks after reaping. We'd go down the lines of stucks giving each a kick along the way with our cairn terrier, Trixie, taking delight in killing rats. One time, he killed eleven rats along a hedge in a short space of time. I was with Austin Fagan that time a rat got Trixie by his nose, and I stood on the rat's body until it let go. When it let go, Trixie tore the rat apart. I had warned Austin to get out of the way, but he wasn't quick enough. He ended up with a bit of the rat's gut wrapped around his hand. Austin was so anxious to get rid of the blood, we had to stop at the Ragwell to clean up on the way home. I laughed as he pumped away and arrived home soaked.

When one of the Fagan lads was working for the Shackletons, he was given a gun with a rifle barrel. My pal, Austin Fagan, used to bring it along when we went out for shooting rabbits and that gave me an interest in guns. My father bought me an air rifle the next Christmas. By the age of fourteen, I had four air rifles, which wasn't uncommon back then. Despite the Firearms Act 1925, enacted to govern gun control following the Civil War, I never had a gun licence growing up. You only needed a gun licence if the inside of the barrel had 'rifling' in it, but the barrels of all my guns were smooth. I'd leave one gun propped up against the wall in the kitchen and a box of pellets beside it. My mother used to call me when she spotted a rat in the ditch and off I'd go to shoot it. The minute I'd pick up the

My favourite gun – me and my sister, Dolores. Courtesy Reynolds Family Private Collection.

gun, Trixie went mad, because he loved hunting. One day I picked up the gun and Trixie came outside with me. I stopped when I realised I'd forgotten my box of pellets, but Trixie ran back inside and brought them out in his mouth. And they say dogs are dumb?

In the 1970s, gun licensing requirements tightened considerably with the Troubles in Northern Irleand - handguns, high-calibre rifles and repeating shotguns were effectively banned. Gun owners were not permitted to leave a gun in a car and they were obliged to hand any guns into the local police station when they were going away. Renewal of gun licences required an application to a Garda Superintendent, accompanied by written letters from two landowners permitting you to shoot on their land. When further requirements were imposed with the escalation of crime involving firearms, the increasing restrictions made keeping a gun for sport more onerous. By the time the law came in obliging gun-owners to keep guns secured in a locked cabinet, I no longer had a gun.

The demesne at Luttrellstown was a favourite hunting ground, mainly for rabbits. It covered a vast area so it was difficult to keep intruders out and entry wasn't policed like at Knockmaroon or Farmleigh. My usual companions for these forays were Austin Fagan from the Sandpits Cottages and Dick Sullivan from Diswellstown cottages, together with a series of dogs, our own and others we gathered along the way. At first, other dogs barked at our dogs but when encouraged by Dick Sullivan's low whistle, they'd join the team. Dick had a great way with dogs. First off, we used to go up the Carpenterstown Road to Mooney's gate and whistle for 'Woopsie' Mooney. Woopsie was an unexcitable dog that never wagged its tail, great for catching rabbits. Then we cycled down Canon's Lane to Porterstown where about four or five dogs joined us from Porterstown cottages.

Like a military operation, we manoeuvred bicycles, dogs and ourselves over the wall and into the castle grounds. Here's how it worked. One of us got on top of the wall and straddled it while the other held a bicycle up high - the bike was hauled up and then lowered to the ground. Next, we'd whoosh one the dogs up one-by-one and they'd help by scrabbling up the stone wall. Once the dogs were over, we hopped over ourselves. An area called 'the gallops' in the castle grounds was full of thorny bushes, abundant with rabbits.

One memorable day was when Dick Sullivan came along. By the time we got near Luttrellstown Castle, we had about eight dogs running alongside us, all friendly by then and rearing to go. A man called Casey, who owned an accountancy firm, lived across the road from the castle. He had three dogs; a dalmation, a Labrador, and a pet greyhound, who was a marvellous hunter. Casey's dogs came running when Dick Sullivan whistled. As usual, we went to 'the gallops' where we ran the rabbits out for the greyhound. On the way home, we had about six rabbits. The dogs alongside us were panting and covered in mud. Mr. Casey came out from behind his gate and shouted, '*you have no business taking my dogs.*' We denied it, claiming *the dogs* followed *us*. Anyway, the Fagans and the Sullivans had a good feed of rabbits that evening. My mother hated the taste of rabbit and refused to cook them. Dick Sullivan kept his whistle softer the next time. Dick went to the Lucan Technical School in the opposite direction and went on to work at a mill in Lucan and settled there. We lost touch when he married.

Another favourite hunting ground was Leixlip Castle, where the land was let out during the war, although it was farther afield. Back then, it was owned by a man called W.J. Kavanagh whose wife was a former Dawn Beauty Queen, the equivalent of Miss Ireland today. As well as being a businessman, he was also a racehorse trainer. He had a great horse called 'Stroller' who won a lot of big races.

Another pursuit was ferreting. Paddy Malone, Austin Fagan and myself pooled a few shillings and bought three ferrets which we kept in a hay shed at Malone's farmyard. The two females - does – were fawn in colour and fit in the palm of your hand; the fierce black polecat was twice their size. We'd put the ferrets into a cage and either stick to Malone's fields or head to Leixlip Castle in a pony and trap. At Leixlip Castle, we'd cover over rabbit holes with our nets in the widest possible area and when the nets ran out, we'd cover more rabbit holes with rocks. Next, we'd let the ferrets out of the cage - they'd rush into the burrows causing mayhem. You'd hear the kerfuffle above ground as the rabbits squealed and went running in all directions. The black polecat was by far the best at ferreting but he was vicious, ready to attack Malone's dog or even humans. Once the ferrets sucked blood from the rabbits, they'd go asleep, so getting the ferrets back was often a problem, especially the polecat. We read up about ways to draw out the ferrets. Sometimes, we'd dip brown paper in a substance that we bought at the chemist's. We'd light the brown paper and hold it at the entrance to a rabbit hole and blow it into the burrow to smoke the ferrets out. The best way to draw the polecat out involved advance planning. We'd separate him from the females about two days before hunting and keep him apart from the females when they were caged. As soon as we put a doe at the mouth of a burrow, the polecat would launch himself out at such speed that you'd need to have a sack ready to throw over him. Then it was a case of holding him by the neck and getting him into the sack head first to avoid serious injuries.

Everybody gave a hand bringing home the hay, stacking it and drawing it home on a bogie, which was a flat cart pulled by a horse. Anyone who has experience of a travelling on a horse and cart knows that the horse's pace quickens on its homeward-bound journey. Trotting faster and faster and yet faster still, it turns into a gallop on the final stretch, so much so that when it turns in the gate to home, there's a risk of the cart turning over or hitting off the pillars.

A particular incident happened in Leixlip, after Mr. Malone had harvested the grain he had planted. He gave Paddy the job of removing the stucks. We took a bogie each and hitched them up - Paddy took the Malone's vicious mare, which was a huge horse, hard to handle. I took Malone's big grey horse. In Leixlip Castle, we stacked the bogies high with straw and tied the loads down with ropes. When we set off for home, Paddy went first with the mare and flew up Captain's Hill, which is very steep. I followed suit but when the grey horse neared the corner half way up, it started slipping. The horse was struggling, slipping back further and further, until it eventually collapsed onto his knees. While it was slipping, it had managed to veer off the hill and came to rest at a farm gate. The poor horse was there panting in the gateway, its shins bloodied. I was wondering what to do when Paddy appeared down the hill on foot, having left the mare tied up at the top. We were there encouraging the grey horse and thought it was the end of him, but before we could do a thing, he got up again and with a miraculous force, made a run up the hill dragging the huge load to the top.

When I bought a 250cc motorbike, it was a great source of pleasure as well as a means of transport, but it had its risks. One wet and misty night, my mother asked me to go over to Aunt Jen in Ashtown with a message. As I took the sharp turn towards the Ashtown gate of the Phoenix Park, the motorbike skidded, hit the kerb and took off. It shot right over the railings, narrowly missing a few trees and it crashed to the ground. There I was in a heap but with no bones broken; the bike was on its side and the engine was still running. I brushed myself down, hopped on the bike and continued on. My mother hated the motorbike and rightly so, but despite having a few motorbike accidents, I never got a single cut.

17.
RELIGION

The Roman Catholic Church now has five parishes serving the area: Blanchardstown parish, Castleknock parish, Corduff parish, Laurel Lodge parish and Navan Road parish. In the Church of Ireland, merger, rather than sub-division, has been the practice nationally, due to dwindling numbers. Thus three civil parishes in the area merged to form the 'United Parishes of Castleknock and Mulhuddart with Clonsilla.'

Religion played a huge part in the life of Irish people but it was also the source of a divide even down to village life where one was expected to mix with one's own brethren. During the Reformation, Protestant churches were built in the towns but Catholic churches could only be built outside towns; this still marks the position of many churches in today's villages. The Protestant Church was always at the core of Castleknock village, whereas the nearest Catholic churches were in Porterstown and Blanchardstown, until a new Catholic church, Our Lady Mother of the Church, opened near Beechpark Avenue in 1983, followed by St. Thomas the Apostle Church in Laurel Lodge which opened in 1993.

The Viceregal Lodge in the Phoenix Park was in the Parish of Castleknock. It was home to the Lord Lieutenant, who held the highest office in the land until 1922. Protestant Church services in Castleknock were attended by the Lord Lieutenant, the Chief and Under Secretaries and other dignitaries, together with the local gentry including for example, the Brooke family, the Holmpatrick family and the Guinness family. They were accustomed to socialising together at events - hunts, balls, the Royal Dublin Horse Show and many were members of the same clubs, such as the Kildare Street Club. Although this provided a level of cohesion among Protestants, it also cultivated a natural divide that extended beyond church attendance to school attendance and social structure. The manner in which the Catholic church ran its parishes also cultivated a divide in that the parish priest controlled the school and the parish hall, which was usually the only venue for socialising and also, the Catholic Young Men's Society (CYMS). Another factor which inhibited intermingling was the *ne temere* rule where the Catholic Church obliged non-Catholics marrying Catholics to undertake that children of the marriage would be brought up in the Catholic faith.

Catholics were obliged to go to Mass at least once a week and to confession at least once a month. It was usual for Catholics to bless themselves by making a sign of the cross when they were passing a church or a funeral. No one missed Mass or even a church ceremony, and nobody left early. One lady from the Lower Road, who always dressed smartly in a black tailored coat and hat, was always first up for Communion at Porterstown Chapel.

Every Saturday evening there was a line-up for Confession in the church, in readiness for being 'free of sin' before Sunday Mass. Generally, the Confession box had three compartments. The priest seated himself behind a curtain in the middle compartment and slid across a wooden door to one side compartment in order to hear the list of sins from the kneeling penitent through a metal grille.

Holy Water receptacle (Holy Water was blessed and brought back from Knock and Lourdes). Courtesy Little Museum of Dublin.

"Bless me Father, for I have sinned. My last confession was three weeks ago."

Mumbling prayers as he made a sign of the cross in the air constituted absolution and then the priest meted out penance.

"Say two Hail Marys, four Our Fathers and a decade of the Rosary, and beg God for forgiveness. In ainm an Athar agus an Mhic agus an Spioraid Naoimh, Amen." (In the name of the Father, the Son and the Holy Spirit. Amen)

Meanwhile, a second penitent was kneeling in the other side compartment waiting his turn.

Although it was a whispered exchange through closed doors, those waiting in the pews could fairly well get the drift of what was being said. Even if they couldn't quite hear, they often gauged from the raised voice of the priest or the reaction of the penitent emerging from the side compartment whether he'd had much sin on his soul. Another pointer was the length of the penance the penitent had to undertake while kneeling at a pew.

Of course, there were 'easy' priests who were light on penance and others who could very well shout at you in the darkness when you revealed your evil nature. One pal of mine was shook after a severe reprimanding at Confession. He told me he went on to Confession in a different church afterwards but the priest there was more lenient. I asked him how come.

"*I told him a pack of lies,*" he replied.

Back then, the priest used to say Mass with his back to the congregation, except when he moved to the pulpit to deliver a sermon. The sermon might very well involve the priest thumping the pulpit with a rousing sermon for half to three quarters of an hour, breathing hell, fire and damnation and warning us of the evil that would befall us for breaches and sins.

After Christmas, Easter and in October, the 'dues' were read out from the altar at Sunday Mass. Starting with the highest donor, the priest read out publicly the names of donors and the amount of their donation, from the top all the way down. It was a source of shame to some who could ill afford to donate, especially when the priest skipped mention of their house, which indicated no donation at all had been made. I remember well those who ranked at the top of our list which always included '*Maxwell Arnott – five pounds*.' Mr. Arnott always made a donation although he was not a Catholic.

Another status marker was 'the silver collection,' where those who had made a 'silver' donation were permitted to enter through the side entrance door to the church, while the 'copper collection' crew were only permitted to enter via the main entrance at the back. It is hard to believe that a gated rail divided worshippers belonging to the 'silver' and 'copper' collections and this was strenuously policed by a volunteer, as was a gated rail further up the church which divided the priest from the congregation. One local lady who was a particularly avid Mass-goer used to open both gates and march right up to the altar, much to the consternation of all in attendance.

In keeping with tradition, men assembled for a chat outside the church gates after Mass. You were expected to fast before Mass, in preparation for receiving Holy Communion, so the pangs of hunger stretched as you walked home afterwards in eager anticipation of a fry, accompanied by toast and a big pot of tea.

In addition to Mass on Sunday, other church attendances were required. Devotions in May or October entailed devotion to certain saints, the Virgin Mary being the most prominent example. Holy Days of Obligation, major feast days in the Catholic Church, had to be observed. Lent brought the Stations of the Cross and Holy Hour, which was on the first Friday of every month. For Sodality, held on the first Sunday of every month and meant for attaining piety, parishioners were broken into groups called 'guilds.' On Ash Wednesday, the priest applied ashes to the foreheads of the congregation, to symbolise the dust from which we are made, speaking the words, *"Remember that you are dust, and to dust you shall return."* It was permissible for ashes to be brought home to a sick person. The Easter ceremonies included Palm Sunday and Good Friday, which was an exceptionally quiet day when no shops or pubs were open, a day of contemplation. Hot cross buns featured on the menu on Good Friday. The Feast of Corpus Christi in late May brought the place to standstill as everybody took part in the procession. The Rosary was recited, hymns were sung and Benediction took place. When there was Rosary or Benediction, everybody stayed until the last hymn had been sung. We had Benediction with the Blessing of the Blessed Sacrament accompanied by singing and the release of incense from a thurible.

Apart from being baptised and christened, young Catholics also had to undergo the sacraments of Holy Communion and Confirmation which were quite onerous. At the age of seven you were decked out for First Communion or if you were a younger sibling, you inherited hand-me-down 'good clothes' to wear. Few had cameras, so photographs of these occasions were rare, as were

My sister Maureen making Confirmation and me making Communion c. 1934. Excuse the child's scribbles. Photograph taken by local photographer, Jim Murray. Courtesy Reynolds Family Private Collection.

celebratory meals. Afterwards, those clothes were kept for best until they were either worn out or passed on to a sibling or cousin.

Intending Communicants had to participate in a May procession which involved a slow walk behind three priests under a canopy – one priest came from Porterstown and two came from Blanchardstown. The procession left Porterstown and went along the Clonsilla Road culminating in a Mass at Blanchardstown church. Another procession, 'Forty hours for the Exposition of the Blessed Sacrament' took the same route. Scouts in full uniform had to attend for the duration of the ceremony. A few scouts were detailed to stand still on the church altar - the detail was changed hourly.

Children between the ages of about eleven and fourteen from Castleknock, Clonsilla and the wider the locality were all confirmed in Blanchardstown. For months beforehand, you'd be dreading the thought of the bishop going from pew to pew asking religious questions, in case you did not know the answer and brought shame on the teacher and the school. Both Communion and Confirmation brought forward gifts of medals, rosary beads and prayer books and, it was hoped, the gift of some money.

Some became altar boys after Communion and served Mass at St. Mochta's Church in Porterstown until about the age of thirteen. They wore white starched surplices with a red soutane. Father O'Neill was always asking me to become an altar boy, but I managed to side-step that one neatly. Altar boys had three main duties, serving to the 'right,' serving to the 'left,' and ringing the bell. Some used to dash up to the church early so they could choose the bell. Altar boys had the honour of holding the bishop's mitre or crozier during confirmation ceremonies.

On Sundays, it was a sin to do manual labour and generally, shops only opened for a short time in the morning so people could buy newspapers and provisions. You had to observe the rule of abstinence – no meat on Fridays - many Catholics designated Friday a 'fish' day. Over time and with the decline of the hold the Catholic Church had on parishioners, these rules were observed less and less and many are now gone.

St. Brigid's Church, Blanchardstown, was the main church in the parish, whereas St. Mochta's church in Porterstown was known as 'a chapel of ease,' to assist with serving the large congregation in the parish. There was no Catholic church in Castleknock at the time. However, there was a local belief that priests in need of a rest were sent to Porterstown. Father O'Neill was okay but there was a Father Crosby who was tall and good-looking with black curly hair. When Father Crosby failed to show for Mass, the congregation used to wait and wait and finally they'd send an emissary to rouse the priest but either he wouldn't open the door or he'd shout, *"I'm not coming out."* Sometimes the congregation sent for a priest in Castleknock College to say Mass and waited in the church until the priest arrived. On occasions when Father Crosby refused to come out, one parishioner, Mr. Dunne, who lived near the Woolly Corner, stood in for the priest at Friday night Devotions or he read out the Stations of the Cross. Father Crosby was succeeded by the very nervy Father O'Rourke who was a nice man, a pipe smoker. Father O'Rourke used to fiddle with the book on the lectern in the pulpit and he once

St. Mochta's, Priest's House, Porterstown. Courtesy Reynolds Family Private Collection.

let it drop from a height to the floor. He supervised dances at the local hall and used a stick to come between any couple caught jitterbugging.

The long arm of religion stretched into people lives to the extent that during Lent, all entertainment was cancelled. This was made possible because the parish priest usually controlled the parish hall or community hall, which in our case, was the CYMS in Porterstown. In any event, the moral police in the area would not approve of any gaiety during Lent. Nobody required notice of this because the practice prevailed throughout Ireland whereby no dances were held during Lent apart from those which ran on a commercial basis in Dublin city centre. It was usual that the church provided the land on which the hall was built but the parishioners raised the funds to build it. It seems that the priests retained ownership of such halls as some were put up for sale and sold off by the parish priest without any recourse to the parishioners.

Retreats were regular feature in the parish. I remember going on a Sodality excursion by train to Tramore in Co. Waterford which was uneventful, except on the way back. One chap decided that it would be easier to simply get off the train at Castleknock instead of having to reach the terminus in the city centre and then have make his way home. He lived along the railway line so he pulled the communication cord about a mile back at Clonsilla, knowing well that it took a considerable distance to stop the train. When the train stopped, he hopped off and went home through the fields. Although misuse of the communication cord was prohibited back then, there wasn't the same threat of hefty fines for such behaviour.

Weddings at the church were a commonplace sight. The grooms generally wore suits and brides wore dresses in white or cream, but many wore a simple suit. Buttonhole carnations with stems wrapped in tinfoil were the order of the day for the wedding party. In advance of the marriage ceremony, the church required formal notification of the intended marriage. Marriage banns were either posted on the noticeboard or read out from the altar in order to notify the public and ensure that neither party had been married previously. Couples could pay a fee not to have the banns read out and this became a snobbery thing as couples who didn't pay the fee were perceived as poor.

The marriage ceremony took place in early morning, hence the term wedding 'breakfast,' which was usually hosted in hotels such as the Harcourt Hotel or Jury's Hotel. Mostly, the guest list was confined to immediate or extended family. Outside the church, people threw confetti in dolly mixture colours over the couple, rather than showering with them with rice for good luck, as they did elsewhere. Honeymoons were usually a few days long and spent in Ireland - getting the train to Drogheda, Arklow or Belfast was not unusual. Our honeymoon to London by plane was considered exotic. As few new houses were built until the late 1950s and few local authority homes were available, many couples moved in with their parents after the honeymoon.

The 'churching' ceremony still existed for Catholic women who had given birth – they were considered too unclean to participate in Mass and religious ceremonies. Following the birth of a child, women attending the ceremony started on their knees either at the back of the church or from a side door. They inched their way forward to the altar – still on their knees - where the priest holding a candle performed a 'cleansing' ceremony and blessed them, after which they were deemed to be 'purified.'

'Quarter Time' was a four-times-a-year rite where abstinence from eating meat on Friday was extended to Wednesdays too. Fully aware of this, the shopkeepers used to stock extra eggs during quarter time. The prohibition on chewing the Eucharist and touching the Eucharist eventually went and Sodality went by the wayside altogether.

Even in death, a microcosm of 'difference' prevailed between the religions. In Castleknock's Protestant graveyard, Protestants were buried to the right and Catholics to the left. Going to funerals on the way home from school was something to do, a ghoulish interest. When we were ten or eleven, we often came across a funeral around three in the afternoon in the Protestant church and we'd shuffle into the midst of the congregation to see the coffin, out of morbid curiosity.

Once a family member died, a notice with a black border and sometimes, a black ribbon, was placed on the front door. After the doctor and priest had left, the deceased was laid out in 'best' clothes under a fresh white sheet and the house was cleaned in readiness for visitors. Relatives and neighbours helped the bereaved with arrangements and often baked a cake or provided ready-made meals. When the coffin was leaving the house, neighbours closed their curtains out of respect. Catholics in the area were generally brought to Porterstown Church and the coffin placed up at the altar rails, much like it happens today. The funeral procession often travelled past the deceased's home, where it paused for a few minutes. As well as conducting ceremonies for the dying and dead, priests also had a role in comforting the relatives, paying them house visits. Although wakes were commonplace outside Dublin, I first attended one as an adult. When an uncle of a pal died in Wexford, I drove him down for the wake. His uncle, a farmer, was in a coffin in the middle of the floor and sympathisers were seated on chairs against the walls. It was usual to have refreshments placed on tables around the coffin; sandwiches, cake and bottles of ale or porter.

In the graveyards, withering chrysanthemums in russet or gold in the shape of a cross were a common feature to be replaced at Christmas by a holly wreath. All too often, the faded plastic flowers under glass globes on the graves remained there for ages as nobody wanted to be the one to discard them.

18.
LIFE AFTER NATIONAL SCHOOL

When I was about ten, my parents started gearing me up for secondary school. My mother brought me for an interview to the nearest Christian Brothers School, Brunswick Street. At that stage, I was too young and she was supposed to bring me back when I was older. However, the family were pre-occupied with troubles in the shop after that and as a result, I was never sent to secondary school. After national school, it was off to St. Vincent's, a private college in Mountjoy Square, for almost a full year. Next, I started a general course in book keeping and commerce, Irish, Maths, Art and English at Parnell Square School for about another year.

At Parnell Square, the boys used to wipe the blackboard vigorously to create a puff of dust before the arrival of our elderly English teacher, Miss Lyons. She used to come in and say: "*Open a window you stuffy little creatures. Fox, open a window.*" Tommy Fox was a friend of mine from national school who ended up in my class in Parnell Square School. Art was taught by Miss Morrow and this was one of my strong subjects. A tall man with a moustache called O'Rourke was the examiner for art, a *cigire*, as it is in Irish. By the time he arrived at the end of the year, it was a toss-up between myself and Maurice Kane from Rush as to whose art work was best. Maurice won – he was a sound guy who also happened to be the best at everything.

On Saturdays, we had to go to Bolton Street for woodwork with Mr. Aungier. As well as theory, Mr. Aungier assigned practical tasks, such as making a dovetail joint from a length of wood. Each pupil had to secure a suitable piece of timber from a length to carry out the task. As soon as an assistant arrived with the lengths of wood, there was a run on clean pieces of wood without knots. Mr. Aungier was full of sarcasm as he strolled about the class supervising the task. From time to time, he picked up a badly done piece and smashed it off the workbench and simply walked on.

At one stage, my father was going to fix me up with a job as a commercial traveller and he took me to meet a man in that line of work. I was put off by the idea of being on the road all the time and having to stay overnight in far-flung places. Later on, my father came home from work and told me he'd been talking to a man who could get me in to serve my time as a fitter. *"What kind of a job is that?"* I said, thinking it was something to do with tailoring. *"Working in the railway."* It was difficult to secure an apprenticeship at that time if your father hadn't been in the trade so it was considered a privilege if you got fixed up and it cost money too, an extra burden on a family. My father told me he knew a man with influence who could help to get me in. He brought me for an interview with the manager of Inchicore Works. That was how things were done back then.

Having paid a fee, I started a five-year apprenticeship with the Great Southern Railway in 1943 along with six others. Everybody worked a five-and-a-half-day week, to include a half-day on Saturday from 8.00 a.m. to 12.30 p.m. Two years into my apprenticeship, the one-week holiday entitlement was extended to two

Holiday advertisement. Courtesy Little Museum of Dublin.

weeks. Only then did going away on holiday become a regular feature of life.

We were obliged to gain experience in different areas of the 'Works' so we were moved around every couple of months. Some jobs were indoors and more 'cushy' while others involved outdoor work or getting into large pipes or holes in the ground. In addition, there were 'good' and 'bad' bosses whose reputations carried, so many apprentices had misgivings about where they might be sent. Apprentices had to do stints in places such as 'the machine shop,' the 'erecting shop,' where major maintenance work took place, and the 'running shed,' which handled 'running' engines, hot off the tracks for minor repairs, usually leaks. Some maintenance involved work on the largest engines ever to run in Ireland, the *Maedb*, the *Macha* and the *Tailte*, steam locomotives built at Inchicore Works just before I started.

The erecting shop comprised three gigantic hangars up to two-storey roof height, with cranes running up and down along rails on both sides to carry materials from one location to another. Machinery moved overhead constantly with the crane driver receiving hand signals as to what was to be moved and where it was to be placed. The crane hovered, lowered a hook to pick up the chain around an item and then hoisted it to a drop-off point. Some of the engines were pre-1900 but still going strong. A maintenance record was kept to routinely schedule engines for overhaul.

A complete overhaul meant the engine being stripped down and the parts dispatched to various places for maintenance work. The boiler was taken away to the boiler house for testing and repair, wheels went to 'the wheel gang' and pistons went to the machine shop. All these pieces of work took weeks to complete before the engine was ready to be re-built.

Once I was under the wing of Mick from Cork, a fitter in the erecting shop, he became a bit of a father figure. Every time I was instructed to move, Mick told me to stay where I was and he'd square it up – Mick was in the Works for years and knew all the foremen. Towards the end of my apprenticeship, I was sent to the running shed. The chap who ran it was used to a frenetic pace - engines pulled in all the time for quick repair and then back onto the tracks. One snowy day, I was sent off with an old timer who always wore a soft hat; he had a helper who looked just as old. From experience, I knew this meant me doing all the work. The job involved changing a broken spring on a still-hissing engine. I was freezing cold on the snowy track, with drops of boiling water falling onto my head as I hammered away to knock out a pin. There and then, I decided that the Works was not for me in the long term.

While serving their apprenticeship, apprentices to the fitting trade had to attend Bolton Street College of Technology three nights a week for five years. It was no mean feat, cycling home after a full day's work at Inchicore Works, cycling back into Bolton Street for classes and then home again in all weathers. Apprentices who excelled in exams at Bolton Street could avail of an opportunity to do Engineering at Trinity College but the required standard was difficult to attain without the benefit of a secondary education. Not all of us who started together finished our apprenticeships - one dropped out and another died of T.B.

The end of the steam era led to some dereliction within the Works. New diesel-engined trains gradually edged out the steam locomotives. As people bought cars, many of the railways were going out of business, so the Government nationalised all the railways and bus companies and called the new company Coras Iompar Eireann (CIE).

The workplace was less concentrated on health and safety in the 1940s, so between my various jobs and active after-work pursuits, I got toes broken and various gashes over the years. A few bad cuts on one leg became ulcerated, requiring regular attendances with the jubilee nurse for dressings. When the dressings were proving unsuccessful, the nurse wanted me to go for a further consultation, but instead I cured them myself with boric (acid) powder, great stuff that is now outlawed. Another time, when my finger kept bealing with an awfully painful cut, Dr. Lavelle sent me into Mercer's Hospital. Having just missed the surgeon who had gone on rounds, I caught up with the surgical team on a ward. The surgeon glanced at the wound, turned to his houseman and told him to fix up an appointment because he might have to 'lop off' the top of my finger. I still have that finger because I never turned up for the appointment. Back then, people relied on home remedies such as bread poultices, used to draw pus from a wound – the bread was soaked in hot water and wrapped tightly in muslin. A typical antiseptic for bathing cuts was to put a few permanganate crystals into water which then turned purple. Another one was '*Pink Healing Ointment*,' which was bubblegum-pink in colour. People used laxatives to keep themselves 'right,' like *Senekot* capsules or syrup of figs or *Andrews Liver Salts*, a fizzy drink. *Vaseline* was used for everything from sunburn to consumption.

The rest of my working life I spent in paper mills, mostly at Clondalkin Paper

Mills, a fortuitous choice, as that was where I met my wife Gertrude, who worked in the office.

As for my siblings - my eldest sister, Maureen, worked in our shop until she married. My sisters, Carmel, Dolores and Geraldine attended the Dominican nuns for secondary schooling in Eccles Street and afterwards, they all went on to do office work. In accordance with the practice, women had to leave on marriage, with few exceptions. Carmel worked for the Electricity Supply Board and later on, at Michael Walsh Travel. Dolores worked for CIE. Geraldine worked on a dental survey on children's teeth which involved travelling around the country and she later worked for Michael Walsh Travel too. All three travelled abroad when few did so, to Rome and the Holy Land. As Geraldine worked at the travel agency for a number of years, she got to more exotic locations such as the Lebanon and Acapulco before she settled down to married life in Co. Louth. My brother, Noel, attended the Christian Brothers at O'Connell School in the city and after a start at making blinds and a stint in England, he returned to work and live in Co. Meath. The rest of us settled within three miles of home.

19.
POLITICS

There were three political parties when I was growing up— Fine Gael, Fianna Fail and Labour. Until 1932, Cumann na nGaedheal ruled as a minority government, but having merged with two smaller groups, the party became known as Fine Gael. From the formation of the first Fianna Fáil government in 1932, the Fianna Fáil party was continuously in office for almost sixteen years, up to 1948. Most families supported a specific political party and this information was known to all and sundry, including the politicians who banked on their votes. Generally, politicians' sons took over from their fathers - there were few female politicians and not much has changed in Ireland in that regard.

To drum up votes coming up to an election, politicians and fellow party men undertook election tours, canvassing house-to-house by car and on foot. Some political meetings were attended by hundreds of people. Torch-lit processions involved party supporters marching behind a colourful party banner. They soaked sods of turf in oil, placed the sods on top of pitchforks, then lit the sods, before raising them upright.

On Sundays, candidates were outside the church after Mass. They used to stand up on a flat-backed truck, megaphone in hand, addressing popular issues and pontificating about their achievements, public positions they had held and their involvement in voluntary organisations. Their faithful followers stayed to hear them out. The cants became familiar as they made promise after promise, looking for your vote - elections could be won or lost on the strength of a speaker's oratory.

The banter was often accompanied by music from a local band. Some bands backed certain candidates and if there was more than one band in an area, it roused excitement if they were backing opposing candidates, with marching and counter-marching going on. Victory was met with scenes of jubilation - the tricolor waving, speeches of gratitude, cheering and shouting. In some places, church bells tolled and tar barrels and bonfires were lit in celebration. With the arrival of television in 1965, candidates paid more attention to party political broadcasts and radio and TV time was allotted by agreement.

My earliest memory of politics is getting the day off school when an election took place, as the schools were used as polling stations. My parents were staunch Fianna Fail supporters and my father was secretary of the local Cumann in Blanchardstown, having been a member of the old I.R.A. in 1922. He was very actively involved in the Fianna Fail party during the 1930s and 1940s. His duties included taking the minutes at party meetings, writing reports and meeting politicians. On polling days, he called around to houses ensuring voters had a lift to the polling station, as lack of transport and even the weather could influence the turnout on voting day. As politics took up so much of his time he eventually had to abandon it.

One time I spotted a notice in the newspaper whereby anybody who had been involved in the Nationalist movement was entitled to a medal, but they had to claim it by a certain date. When I mentioned it to my father, he had no interest in a medal, but he changed his mind when I persuaded him that it might be of future benefit to my mother, in the form of a pension. I drove him to his former Commandant in Clonsilla, who vouched for him. He duly got his medal but no pension came with it.

In the 1980s, I remember the late Brian Lenihan Senior canvassing in the area. As he was approaching our house, our windows were open and we heard him say, *'Give that house a miss, they're Fianna Fail. We're running out of time.'*

20.
NIGHT LIFE

Before my parents came to live at Carpenterstown, a club house had been built by some of the Reynolds' men and men from the Sandpits to one side of our triangular front garden. The 'hut,' as we called it, became the focal meeting point in the locality for card players. When more cottages were built at nearby Diswellstown, the hut got a revived use. A local theatre group, *The Gleann Dubh Players*, used it for rehearsals and many locals became involved in dramatics. Other dramatic societies in the area were *The Magnet* and *The Clonsilla Players*. They mainly put on Irish plays. The hut was later widened and extended at the back. At that time, it had a skittles table, which was like a snooker table. On occasion, bands came to play and sometimes, the hut was used for band practice. Now and again, the hut was used as a function room for parties. I remember high jinks at one party when they locked me into a room with a woman. Another time, they blindfolded me and made me feed jam to a girl.

The Reynolds family had a good relationship with those using the hut but eventually it became a nuisance due to noise levels, the presence of crowds and various strangers wandering in and out past our place. As the numbers using it dwindled and it became more decrepit, we were hoping its use would tail off. Then the scouts took it over and it went through another revival with Jack Lovely from the bottom of the Glen as the scoutmaster. When Jack looked to extend the hut further in 1969, it marked its natural end. The scouts got permission to use the smaller hall in Porterstown, which they use to this day. Some bands continued to practice in the hut from time to time but eventually, it fell into complete disuse. The hut was eventually taken down in the late 1960s.

There was very little to do at night in the area, so people were accustomed to

Scout's Hall, Clonsilla (formerly home to the CYMS), 2017. Courtesy Reynolds Family Private Collection.

cycling some distance for entertainment. A building with a corrugated tin roof at the back of The Thatch shop in Clonsilla, owned by the Horan family, was used as a dancehall, plays and showing films. Other cinemas within cycling distance included the Ritz, behind the Mullingar House pub in Chapelizod – the hall still exists - and the Premier Cinema in Lucan. Two brothers called Rice operated 'tent' cinemas – one was in the square alongside 'McCarthy's Lane' in Lucan, the other was beside the garage on the main street in Blanchardstown. The tents were a timber and canvas structure erected on a mud floor, with wooden sides and a tent roof. The bench seats were cheaper because they had no back – they were about half the price of the more sophisticated wooden seats. A projector was operated from the back onto a screen in front of the audience. Generally, they showed black and white cowboy films. Once everybody was seated, the lights went out and the film started. After a while, there was a break so that the projectionist could change the reel. Cheers went up when the baddie was captured or the hero was saved. As smoking was the norm, a haze of smoke rose up to join the tunnel of light from the projector.

In his squeaky voice, Mr. Rice used to stand on a bench about half way through the evening to announce forthcoming films and sometimes, a double feature. When there was no double feature, they often showed what we called 'shorts,' starring *Charlie Chaplin*, *Laurel and Hardy*, the *Three Stooges*, *Buster Keaton* or

Tony Reynolds

Horan's Hall at the back of The Thatch. Courtesy Reynolds Family Private Collection.

the *Marx Brothers*. Posters were pasted up in the area to announce forthcoming films. As we always took posters for our shop window, we got a few free cinema tickets. Later on, the Grove cinema was opened, beside Lucan's Liffey bridge – after it was demolished, a bank and an apartment block were built on this spot.

A pal of mine, Frank McCarthy, lived near the site of the 'tent' cinema in Lucan. When Frank's sister, Sally, was getting married, she asked us to remain on stand-by for lifts home for the girls she had invited to her pre-wedding 'bash.' We were happy to oblige. We arrived back from the cinema and realised we were the only men among a gang-load of women. We both fancied an attractive Maltese girl but unfortunately, her chap then arrived to collect her, so then we put our eyes on two other girls. I fancied a girl that was playing the piano and Frank fancied a girl wearing a white blouse. As luck would have it, we manoeuvred a situation whereby each of us got to leave home the girls of our choice. When I arrived at my girl's house in Donnycarney, a car pulled up behind me, blinding us with its lights – Frank McCarthy's car. It turned out that the two girls we were leaving home were sisters, although they didn't look alike at all. We had a double date following that when we took them to the motorcycling in Skerries.

The cinemas in town, like the Capitol, the Ambassador and the Savoy provided a different experience, often starting with a live stage show or a stand-up comedian followed by the *Pathé News* which in wartime comprised live news reels. Before the feature film got going, they often put on a cartoon show or comedy sketches and showed trailers of films to come. Not all films were shown in one sitting – sometimes they had what we called 'follower-uppers,' where the film cut off at a point of great suspense and you had to see the 'follower-upper' another time to find out what happened. One time I went to a film featuring a pet monkey with Paddy Malone, Jim Malone and Austin Fagan. When a series of mysterious incidents pointed the finger at several suspects, Jim shouted out, '*It was the monkey all the time,*' before he was shushed by the audience.

One night, myself, Tommy Fox and Billy Clarke from Clonsilla, set off on bikes to a dance at Islandbridge. Whizzing down Knockmaroon Hill, Billy had to put his foot to the ground to stop because his brakes were not working. In doing so, he tore the leather sole on his shoe which was left flapping. We made fun of him as he tied a string around it to hold it together. Billy had the last laugh when was the only one of us who got to leave home a girl after the dance – he got a 'leave home,' as we used to say.

My cousin, Tommy Reynolds, was my regular companion for many day-time outings and night-time forays, although he worked away a lot, being in the Meteorological Service. We often went along the coast to Arklow, a holiday mecca at the time. We'd spend the day on the beach, have our tea in Hoyne's Hotel on the Main Street and then make our way to the Marquee dance-hall, which had originally been a tented marquee dance but by that stage, it had become a proper dance-hall.

Tony Reynolds and cousin, Tommy Reynolds at the beach. Courtesy Reynolds Family Private Collection.

Tony Reynolds

Tony Reynolds and cousin, Tommy Reynolds in the Olympic Ballroom, Dublin. Courtesy Reynolds Family Private Collection.

It is hard now to imagine life without television but I do remember the earlier programmes when TV arrived in the 1960s including *Lincoln Vale and the Everglades*, the *High Chaparral*, *Get Smart* and the original version of *Hawaii-Five-O*, which starred Jack Lord in the lead role. I also remember the first continuity announcers, including Gay Byrne's wife, Kathleen Watkins. Kathleen regaled us in a recent TV programme about the trials at Radio Teilifis Eireann when the reception went on the blink, which was a regular occurence. During periods of disturbance, Kathleen was tasked to don another hat and entertain listeners by playing her harp which was always close to hand for this purpose.

21.
GHOSTLY TALES

Like all Irish places, Castleknock was steeped with ghostly lore, often centred on dark and lonely places and most likely precipitated by a fair few drinks in local hostelries. Our Aunt Kitty's husband, Joe Thewlis, was a great storyteller. As he tailored away on garments, he told ghostly tales, keeping listeners in suspense while he threaded a needle or filled his pipe. The tales often came to mind when walking home on a dark and windy night.

Near to the back College gate along the College Road, is a spot where the 'fourteen trees' once stood. The treetops almost join to form a tunnel at this point. This lonely spot was renowned for apparitions of a big black dog and struck such fear into locals that many wouldn't venture past there at all.

On his way home from Castleknock one night, Austin Fagan was passing the 'fourteen trees' when he heard a tap-tapping, like somebody following him. When he stopped, the noise continued on, but when he looked behind him, there was nothing there. However, he soon realised there was a pumping sound coming from the water tower facility on the top of Tower Hill in the College which provided a logical explanation.

Another such place for ghostly appearances is beside White's Gate leading to the Phoenix Park, along 'Weekes's Road' as it was called. A strange thing happened to my father here one night on his way home from work. He had just wheeled his bicycle through the Park gate onto Weekes's Road and stopped to light a cigarette, when he saw what appeared to a big shadowy dog bounding in his direction. He lifted the front wheel of his bicycle and spun it in the direction of the ghostly apparition to shine his lamp on it, but the large shadowy creature passed him by.

Years later, my wife's two uncles came to visit. They mentioned a strange incident as they cycled along Weekes's Road towards town, just before the Park gate, in the very same spot where my father had the strange experience. A large shadowy creature ran between their bikes and they both remarked on the fact that they had seen a ghost.

My father used to bring us to the 'fairy' tree in The Glen. The old tree was right beside the stream and its huge trunk was disfigured by many man-made indentations, one of which we believed was the door to the fairies house, while other markings represented the windows. The tree is now gone.

On their way home from the cinema in Chapelizod one night, my two sisters, Carmel and Maureen, had a strange experience passing Mount Sackville Convent. My sister Carmel was conscious of two nuns walking towards them dressed in white with dark veils and when they'd passed by, she turned her head to look after them. She remarked to my sister Maureen how unusual it was to see nuns out at that hour, because they were generally confined to the convent. She was surprised to find that Maureen had no idea what she was talking about. It made it all the more odd that they were walking close to Farmleigh's Clock Tower at the time, because they'd heard rumours about a banshee in the clock tower, a banshee being a fairy woman who keens to warn of impending death. As many ghostly happenings can often be attributed to alcohol intake, it is important to note that neither of them drank alcohol.

I mentioned previously that a man nicknamed "Skin-the-Goat," real name James Fitzharris, was reputed to have lived in a house in the Strawberry Beds that was said to be haunted. Born in Wexford, Skin-the-Goat became an Irish republican and he worked as a horse and cab driver in Dublin. He was sworn into 'The Invincibles,' a secret society whose aim was to assassinate leading members of the British administration in Ireland. Having served as the getaway jarvey during the assassination of Permanent Under Secretary Thomas Henry Burke and Lord Frederick Cavendish in the Phoenix Park, he was tried and found not guilty of the murders. In a re-trial in May 1883, he was convicted of conspiracy and accessory to murder and sentenced to penal servitude for life but he was later released from prison.

At one stage, my uncle Larry and his wife, Winnie, lived in the house where Skin-the-Goat is reputed to have lived. Situated between Lovelys' home and Tobins' shop, it was a long, single-storey, solidly-built house. It had a clock on the wall with its pendulum hanging close to the floor. I asked my uncle Larry about the house being haunted and at first he said no, but then he recalled one night when he was in bed fast asleep and suddenly, felt himself lifted off the bed and dumped onto the floor. I must add that my Uncle Larry was a modest drinker.

A renowned ghost, the 'White Lady of Castleknock,' is said to appear on Castleknock Hill. This goes back to the sixteenth century and the kidnapping of Eileen, beautiful daughter of a Wicklow Chieftain called O'Byrne, by the notorious John Tyrrell, brother of the sixth Baron of Castleknock. Anticipating violence at the hands of Tyrrell, Eileen is said to have bled to death having opened her veins with a breast pin. The ghost of Eileen, a white-robed female figure is said to move around the Castle walls at night.

> When distant chimes sound midnight hour,
> The spirit pure is seen
> And moving round the lonely tower.
> Looks bright as moonlight beam.
> And as the moonbeams tint the walls,
> And light the turret's crest,
> Twas hence, she says, 'my spirit fled,
> Tis here my bones find rest.
> And here I wander, year by year,
> For such my lot has been,
> But soon at end my penance drear,
> I'll rest in joy unseen.

- From the Nation.

EPILOGUE

People can make or change a village. In Castleknock, I had a place in the community and a unique identity. Everything I knew about nature I learned there – how to catch and scale and gut a fish, how to hold an animal living or dead, how to listen, how families can be affected by illness and tragedy. These things I kept with me always. My instincts were developed and built on for life, at a time when I knew not what lay ahead, good or bad. It is natural, however, that people break away bit by bit and many end up living between two worlds, their childhood home and their new life. Unlike many communities in Ireland, most of the children I grew up with were lucky enough to get work and remain in the greater Dublin area.

As time pushes on, change comes about, and so it did in Castleknock. In the late 1950s, a pocket of development started on the Side Road. The new Beechpark Avenue houses cost IR£1,850, a huge sum at the time. After a short reprieve, development started to burgeon ahead relentlessly as farm after farm was sold on. Lord Iveagh's Farmleigh is now an OPW property enjoyed by the public, Luttrellstown Castle is a high-end hotel and golf club, Castleknock Hotel & Country Club is built on former Laidlaw land, and Diswellstown House is at the centre of a building site. The vicinity of our old place remains relatively pastoral at the present time, largely due to its proximity to the unchanged grounds of Castleknock College and the intact Guinness estates of Knockmaroon and Oatlands and the Glen in between these two estates.

While advances in mechanisation and technology and cars for all brought more comfortable times, a lot was lost, like neighbourliness and closeness to nature. I do not notice the three-storey apartment blocks nor do I know anybody in the new estates. As time goes on, I seem fated to be a stranger among strangers.

Castleknock – Memories of a Neighbourhood

The Castleknock I knew has changed for good, vanished beyond recognition, but the old landscape is imprinted in my mind. While traversing the roads of life, I also traverse the roads of my youth in a different way to newcomers. I pass by a gate or a fence that has not altered and everything is preserved at once in my mind in its former outline, as if time had stood still. Every step I take, past certain places, and past the homes of people who lived there once brings back memories. Many are now gone but not forgotten.

I feel myself called back into the past, to my old life, showing me how far I have travelled and how remote that old way of life has become, but that sense of belonging creeps through me once more. I am once again the schoolboy who did the paper rounds, who hunted and fished and took sheer pleasure in walking the fields with a dog by my side. All those familiar landmarks come to mind – the Glen with its fading heath and bracken, the scent of thickened foliage and the thud-thud of the quarry at the far end, the ever-present clock tower at Farmleigh and the core of Castleknock village. I am carried away to the graveyard in Castleknock where Reynolds lies beside Reynolds, all linked to the same soil and to one another in a community of land and blood. As if it was yesterday, I remember going around by the postbox at the top of the Sandpits Hill on my first day at school and yet nine decades of life have crept by.

Postbox beside old Reynolds family home at the top of Sandpits Hill. Courtesy of Reynolds Private Family Collection.

I think myself back to evenings when I stood at our stone wall, looking over at Castle Hill. As the sun goes down, the crows kick up a cawing racket as they flock over and back between the tall trees, before converging on a roosting spot for the night. I hear the final ring of the till at cashing up time, the light goes off in the shop and the bolt is drawn across for the evening. Our front door opens and emits a fresh channel of light before it closes over.

OTHER READING ABOUT THE GREATER CASTLEKNOCK AREA

Ball, F.E. 1995 (reproduced from 1906 lithograph), A History of the County Dublin: The people, parishes and antiquities from the earliest times to the close of the eighteenth century. Part Fourth. The HSP Library, Dublin.

Brooke, Raymond Frederick, 1961. *The Brimming River*. Published by A. Figgis.

Chapelizod Historical Society, 2010. *Chapelizod Heritage Society Historical Journal*.

Hulgraine, Charles and Mary, 1990. *St. Mochta's Church*.

Joyce, Weston St. John, 1988. (first published 1912) *The Neighbourhood of Dublin*. Published by The Skellig Press, Dublin

Lacey, J., 1999. *A Candle in the Window*. Published by Marino Books, Dublin, an imprint of Mercier Press

Lacey, Jim, 2015. *The Barony of Castleknock*. Published by The History Press Ireland.

McPolin, Donal and Sobolewski, Peter. *Blanchardstown, Castleknock and The Park*, Published by Cottage Hay Publications, Northern Ireland.

Neary, Bernard 2016. *Dublin 7*. Published by The Lilliput Press.

Nolan, Brendan 2006. *Phoenix Park, A History and Guidebook*. Published by The Liffey Press.

O'Driscoll, James. 1977. *Cnucha - A History of Castleknock and District*. Publisher unknown.

Troy, Patrick. 2013. *The Strawberry Beds*. Published by Original Writing Limited, Dublin.

Helpful websites:-

www.duchas.ie

www.niah.ie

https://blanchardstowncastleknockhistorysociety.wordpress.com/

https://irishwaterwayshistory.com/tag/castleknock/

www.fingalcoco.ie

A final word relates to wonderful records available to everybody.

One is the National Inventory of Architectural Heritage (NIAH), which is part of the Department of Arts, Heritage, Regional, Rural and Gaeltacht Affairs, set up in 1990 for the establishment and maintenance of an inventory of monuments, as well as groups of buildings and sites to be protected, which serves as a central record for architectural heritage purposes. www.niah.ie.

A further resource is the local history collection at Fingal Library in Blanchardstown, where monthly meetings of the Blanchardstown-Castleknock Historical Society are also held.

Another great record is the National Folklore Collection, in particular, The Schools Collection, a collection of folklore, old cures and history compiled by schoolchildren and written in their own handwriting in Ireland in the 1930s. The original records held at the Folklore Department in UCD are now available on-line: www.duchas.ie. The contributions from children in the locality are too numerous to include in this book but some readers may be interested to find handwritten contributions from their forebears. The following is a list of children who contributed while at local national schools, but it must be noted that this list might not be exhaustive.

List of names of schoolchildren in the area who contributed to The Schools Folklore Collection c. 1937/1938:

<u>St. Brigid's Castleknock (Mrs. Thornton) – October 1937</u>
Shiela Byrne, Park Villas, Castleknock, aged 10

Ethna Carty, Carpenterstown, aged 15
Marie Cassidy, Rose Cottage, Castleknock, aged 12
Patricia Clarke, Sandpits, Castleknock, aged 11
Winifred Coyle, Castleknock, aged 14
May Doyle, Clonsilla, aged 14
Mary Fagan, Sandpits, Castleknock, aged 14
May Foran, Park Villa, Castleknock, aged 11
Madeline Hughes, Castleknock, aged 12
Rita Hughes, Sally Gardens, Castleknock, aged 13
Rosaleen Hughes, Front Lodge, Knockmaroon, Castleknock, aged 10
Eileen Morrison, Abbey Lodge, Clonsilla, aged 12
Mona O'Reilly, Blanchardstown, aged 12
Rita Purcell, Park Villas, Castleknock, aged 10
Eileen Purcell, Park Villas, Castleknock, aged 8
Peg Reynolds, Park Villas, Castleknock, aged 9
Teresa Segrave, Castleknock, aged 12
Kathleen Stokes, Castleknock, aged 10

<u>S. O'Leary, Castleknock school</u> (unfortunately, no names of pupils who made the contributions are recorded)

Clonsilla – Teacher: M. Ni/ Cholmain
Lizzie Flood, Hartstown, Clonsilla
Michael Flood, Hartstown, Clonsilla
Gretta Hughes, Porterstown, Clonsilla
Josie Keane, Porterstown, Clonsilla
Tommy Lynch
Paddy McNally, Coolmine, Clonsilla
Frank McNally, Coolmine, Clonsilla
Hilda Mooney, Porterstown, Clonsilla
Ita Mooney, Porterstown, Clonsilla
Paddy Mooney, Clonsilla
Sile Ni Ruaidhrc, Clonsilla
Nancy O'Leary

Blanchardstown – Teacher: T. Ruiseal

Carmel Byrne, Blanchardstown
Mary Johnston, Blanchardstown
George Johnston, Blanchardstown
Kitty Smith, Park Villas, Peck's Lane
Mary Smith, Dunsink
James O'Brien, Corduff
Shiela Monahan, Blanchardstown
Jenny Byrne, Blanchardstown
Kathleen Burke, Blanchardstown
N. Conlon, River Road

Thom's Directory

The Thom's Directory of **1923** shows the following property owners resident in Clonsilla and outlines the rateable valuation of their properties:-

Allendale—Vacant £55
Arnott, Maxwell, Greenmount
Balfe, J., farmer, Porterstown £125
Bobbet, W., Hansfield ho, £183 10s.
Clonsilla Church—Rev. H. Browne, M.A., rector
Clonsilla National Schools — Miss May Coll, principal
Cunningham Bros., Kellystown Saw Mills
Daly, James, Hartstown £194
Dewhurst. Mr?, Greenmount £CG
Ends, Mrs. E., Hillside £7 10s.
Geraghty, Thomas, Barberstown £217 10s.
Gore, Hugh, Clonsilla cott. £58 10s.
Graham, Mrs. S., Dolland £57
Hamilton, Major Edmund, Luttrelstown £100
Harford, P., Westmanstown £108 10s. |
Hepworth, Mrs. E., The Lodge
Hilliard, James, Hartstown £194;

Kelly, Major John Upton, D.S.O., Insp., L.G.B., Lohunda-pk £111
Lambert, T. D., M.R.C.V.S., Annfield £44
CLONSILLA.
Lovewell, G. H., provision merchant £18
Lynam, James, Astagob £49
i Lynam, P., Hartstown farm £49 10s.
| Lynam, L., farmer, Porterstown £30
Lynam, C. M,, Barnhill £17 10s.
Mackey, Patrick, Stirling £25
Maher, J. J., Williamstown house £140
Mangan, Jas., builder, Coolmine
Clonsilla Grange £113
Murphy, D., Barnhill £212
O'Neill, John, grocer, etc.
Porterstown R. C. Church — Rev. W. Lenihan, C.C. £7 15s.
Railway Station — Joseph M'Cabe, stationmaster £5
Rooney, Henry, Phibblestown £122 10s.
Shackleton, John, Beech Park £105
Smith, Edward, Mount view £94 10s. and £93 10s.
Smith, John, M.Inst.C.E.I, assistant surveyor, co. Dublin, Kellystown cottage £133
Steeds, Mrs. Agnes, Clonsilla house. £130
Sub-Post Office—Mrs. K. C, Lovewell, sub-postmistress
Watt, Samuel, Hilltown £51

The Thom's Directory of **1927** shows the following property owners resident in Clonsilla and outlines the rateable valuation of their properties:-

Arnott. Maxwell, Greenmount £66
Balfe. J., farmer, Forterstown £12
Bobbett, W., Hansfield house, £183 10s.
Callaghan, John, Hilltov/n
Clonsilla Church—Rev. H. C.
Browne, M.A., rector—res. 6Hatch-street, Dublin
Clonsilla National Schools — Miss May Coll, principal
Cunningham Bros., Kellystown Saw Mills

Daly, James, Hartstown £194;
Dewhurst, Mrs., Greenmount £66
Ennis, Mrs. E., Hillside £7 10s.
Geraghty, Thomas, Barberstown £217 10s.
Gore. Hugh. Clonsilla eott. £38 10s.
Harford, P.. Westmanstown £10S 10s.
Hepworth, Mrs. E. T. M., The Lodge
Hilliard, James, Hartstown £194
King-French, Capt. Michael Dolland £57
Lohunda-park £111
Lambert, Mrs., Annfield £44
Loveweli, G, H., provision merchant £18
Lynam, James, Astagob £49
Lynam, P., Hartstown £49 10s.
Lynam. L.. farmer, Porterstown £30
Lynam, C. M., Barr.hill £17 10s.
Mackey, Patrick, Stirling £25
Maher, J. J., Williamstown house £140
Mangan, Jas., builder, Coolmine
Murphy, D., Barnhill £212
O'Connor, P. M., Laurel cottage
Porterstown R. C. Church — Rev.
W. Lenihan, C.C. £7 15s.
Railway Station — Joseph M'Cabe, stationmaster £5
Rooney, Henry J., Allendale £55
Rooney, John. Phibblestown house £122 10s.j
Shackleton, John W , Beech Park £165;
Smith. Edward, Mount view £94 10s. and £93 10s. i
Smith, John, M.Inst.C.E.I, asst surveyor, Kellystown cottage £133
Steeds, Mrs. Agnes, Clonsilla house. £130
Sub-Post Office—Mrs. K. C. Lovewell, sub-postmistress £8
Wall. —, Clonsilla Grange £113
Watt, Samuel, Hilltown £51

The Thom's Directory of **1957** shows the following property owners resident in Clonsilla and outlines the rateable valuation of their properties:-

The Cottage—Hon. Mrs. Brinsley-Plunkett £64 10s.
Barnhill—Pringle, Harry £212
Bennett, Thomas, The Bungalow
Byers, Lt.-Col. Rowland M., Clonsilla House £130
Callaghan, John, Hilltown £51
Cannon, Mrs. P., The Lodge £31
Casey, Martin. The Gables £133
Clonsilla, Church of Ireland
Clonsilla National School* —
The Honourable Mrs. Brinsley-Plunket, Luttrellatown Castle £S4
Creaner, Peter, dentist, Earlywood Cottage
Cunningham, Robert £15 15s.
Cunningham Bros., coffin makers & undertakers, Kellystown Saw Mills £111
Cunningham, R, £17 15s.
Dalton. Patrick
Donnelly, B. J. £36 15s.
Everard, J. P.—Barnhill £19 15s.
Hall, Kellystown £15
Hall, Major C. C, Ongar Stud.
Harford, P., Westmanstown £108 10s.
Hughes, C.
Hughes, T.
Harford. M.—St. Mary's
Horan, T.
Horan, J.
Hilltown Stud Farm Limited
Kavanagh, Mrs., Dolland £57
King, Mrs. Anna Maria, Lohunda Park £194
Milltown Stud Farm Limited
Lovewell, George H., provision merchant £18
Luttrellstown Estate Co., The Gardens
Lynam, James, Astagob £491
Lynam, P., Rynella £49 10s.

Lynam, L., farmer. Porterstown £30
McDonald, Thomas, Barberstown Farm £224 10s
Maher, Mrs., Williamstown house £140
Malcolmson, George Villiers, Hartstown £194
Mangan, Patk., builder, Coolmine
Martin, John, Greenmount £66
Martin, P.
Porterstown Catholic Church–
Lady Honor Svejdar, Phibblestown House £122 10s.
Railway station £122 10s.
Redmond, Rev. Fr. J., St. Mochtas, Porterstown £15
Shackleton, David, Beech Park, & Anna Liffey Mills, Lucan
St. Joseph's Home for adult female defectives, under care of Sisters of Charity of St. Vincent de Paul—The Grange £113
Smith, James, Mount view £94 10s. and £91 10s.
Sub-Post Office—Mrs. T. O'Neill, sub-postmistress £8
Svejdar, J., Allendale House, Glenmaroon Estates £217 10s.
Stirling—Vacant £25
O'Rourke, William, Rev., C.C., Astagob £15 £136
Thornton, Robt., Springlawn
Travers. T.
Whyte, Jack, M.R.C.V.S., Annfield

The Thom's Directory of **1957** shows the following resident at Orchard Terrace:

Lynam, L.
Fagan, H.
Downing, Miss
Keating, Miss
Jackson, Miss
Hanlon. Miss
Critchley, Miss
Ward, C.
Thewlis, J., tailor

Mooney, Patrick
Reynolds, James
Smith, —.
Dubbs Cottage
Anderson, —. '

The Thom's Directory of **1923** shows the following residents in Coolmine and the rateable valuation of their properties:-

Balfe, William, farmer, Porterstown
Dillon, Frank, Coolmine cottage, £52 15s.
Dunne, Patrick, Limelawn £78 '5s.
Eager, Robt., Abbey cottage £13
Ellis, Mrs. Woodville
Fagan, Mrs., farmer, Astagob £S<»
Goodwin, M., harness maker. Bloomfield
Hoare, W., Rockfield
Hutton, Mrs., Sheepmore £3t»
Kirkpatrick, Alex, de la Poer.
Captain, Coolmine house £292
M'Donnell, Patk., Woodvilla
Mackey, W., Coolmine
Mangan, J., carpenter
Murphy, Thomas, blacksmith

The Thom's Directory of **1927** shows the following residents in Coolmine and outlines the rateable valuation of their properties:-

Balfe, William, farmer, Porterstown £5
Billon, Frank, Coolmine cottage £52 15s.
Bunne, Patrick, Linielawn £7S 5s.
Eager, Robt., Abbey cottage £13
Ellis, Mrs. Woodville £50
Fagan. Mrs., farmer, Astagob £30
Goodwin, M., harness maker, Bloomfield £6

Hoare, W., Rockfield £43
Button. Mrs.. Sheepmore £36
Kirkp.itrick, Frank, Coolmine house £292
M'Donnell. Patk., Woodvilla £97
Mackey, W.. Coolmine £25
Murphy, Thomas, blacksmith £4

The Thom's Directory of **1957** shows the following residents in Coolmine and the rateable valuation of their properties:-

Balfe, Patrick, farmer £5
Shee, Mrs., Coolmine Cottage £25.15s
Dunne, Patrick, Limelawn £78.5s
Eager, Robert, Abbey Cottage £13
Ellis, Miss, Woodville £50
Astagob – vacant £30
Jellett, Hewitt Barrington, Solicitor, Coolmine House £239
Rockfield – vacant £48
McDonnell, Patrick, Woodvilla £97
Mackey, Miss S.E., Coolmine £25
Malone, James, Sheepmore £36
Matten, J.M., Rockfield, Coolmine
Walsh, Miss, Tresmond £66.10s

ACKNOWLEDGEMENTS

With very special thanks to Fingal County Council for their kind sponsorship of this book which facilitated the acquisition of maps, new photographs and the publication of this book.

Carrowmore Publishing, City Quay, Dublin 2, also deserve a special thanks, in particular, Ronan Colgan, Publishing Director, who has a calm approach in the face of deadlines.

The author gratefully acknowledges the following people and institutions who assisted by pointing me in the right direction or who generously shared information, photographs or permission to reproduce photographs:

Blanchardstown-Castleknock Historical Society.
Daniel O'Neill (Panoramio) for his photograph of Knockmaroon Hill.
Editorial assistants – Mary Reynolds, Mairead Rooney and Cindy Carroll.
Fingal County Council - Enid Bebbington, Senior Librarian.
Fingal Library, Blanchardstown - Yvonne O'Brien, Senior Executive Librarian.
Irish Racehorse Trainers Association – Tony Redmond, who shared the photograph of 'Rasher' Byrne.
Jim Lacey, local historian and author of A Candle in the Window and The Barony of Castleknock.
John Harford, Secretary, Blanchardstown Brass Band, who shared photographs of the band.
National Folklore Collection, Folklore Department, UCD and dúchas.ie. (The Schools Collection).

National Inventory of Architectural Heritage – Willie Cumming, Senior Architectural Advisor,

Department of Arts, Heritage, Regional, Rural and Gaeltacht Affairs.

Ordnance Survey, Phoenix Park – Lucy O'Reilly, copyright and Noel Harrigan for his digitalisation skills.

Patrick Troy, local historian and author of The Strawberry Beds.

Rea Coonan Estate Agents (Maynooth) – Philip Byrne, who shared photographs of Glenmaroon estate.

Sherry Fitzgerald Estate Agents – Julian Cotter, who shared photographs of Oatlands estate.

St. Brigid's National School – Abigail Mooney, who shared old photographs of school and teachers

Trevor White, Director, Little Museum of Dublin, Stephen's Green.

I wish to extend my appreciation to all others who advised and helped as I would like them to feel included in this acknowledgement. I also wish to thank at this stage any photographer with whom I was unable to establish contact in time for this publication.

Note: The author plans to share copies of the many group photographs and photographs of landmarks with the Local History Department in Blanchardstown Library in due course.

ABOUT THE AUTHOR

Tony Reynolds has roots in Castleknock extending back to 1758 and relations scattered throughout the area. His family ran a shop there in the 1930s and the hut alongside the shop was used by the scouts, musical and drama groups, card schools and for dancing. Tony recalls a vibrant past, when Castleknock was mostly farmland, dotted with grand houses. In this book, he brings you on his newspaper rounds and tells you who lived where, who was related to whom and how the community intermingled, a blurring of lines between memoir and local history.